TITANIC

THE LEGEND, MYTHS AND FOLKLORE

Bruce Alpine

RMS.Titanic at Queenstown Harbour, 11 April 1912.
(Now Cobh Harbour)

TITANIC
The Legend, Myths and Folklore.
Bruce Alpine

Copyright © 2013 by Bruce H. Alpine

All rights reserved. No part of this publication may be reproduced, distributed or transmitted in any form or by any means, including photocopying, recording, or other electronic or mechanical methods, without the prior written permission of the publisher, except in the case of brief quotations embodied in critical reviews and certain other noncommercial uses permitted by copyright law. For permission requests, write to the publisher, addressed "Attention: Permissions Coordinator," at the email address below.

queries@brucealpine.com

Book Layout - Bruce Alpine 2016

TITANIC: The Legend, Myths and Folklore

ePub ISBN: 978-1-301-20346-8
Print ISBN: 978-0-9941053-9-4

Acknowledgements

Information pertaining to weather conditions in Southampton on April 10th, 1912 and North Atlantic, is courtesy of National Meteorological Library and Archive (UK)

All reasonable efforts have been made to ensure all images used in **Titanic** the Legend, Myths and Folklore are in the public domain - except, "Fata Morgana," copyright attribution to Mila Zinkova.

Contact The Author:
Bruce-a@brucealpine.com

Discover More Titles From Bruce Alpine:
https://brucealpine.com

About The Author

Bruce Alpine is a science writer based out of the Kapiti Coast in New Zealand. Renowned for his ability to explain complex and technical issues in a way that is both easy to understand and fun to read, Bruce has gained a small but devoted audience since he published his first book, A History Of Life On Earth.

Born in Wellington, New Zealand in 1958, Bruce was the only son of a former college instructor. His mother was born in Britain and immigrated to New Zealand when she was 21. She encouraged Bruce and his three sisters to read often and study hard in school, and when it became clear that Bruce had an affinity for science, she encouraged that too.

Bruce's key interests revolve around the Earth and the life that inhabits it: how it sprang up, how it's come to be the way it is, how it functions now, etc. In addition to his work as a writer, Bruce is employed in the health support industry. He has two children, one son and one daughter, both of whom are grown up.

Contact The Author:

Bruce-a@brucealpine.com

Visit The Website For More Titles Available From Bruce Alpine:

https://brucealpine.com

Contents

Prologue..8
Introduction..12

Chapter 1 ..... The Dream Is Born...........................18
Chapter 2 ..... Launch..31
Chapter 3 ..... Southampton..................................55
Chapter 4 ..... Cherbourg To Queenstown.................81
Chapter 5 ..... To The New World..........................94
Chapter 6 ..... Iceberg, Right Ahead.......................110
Chapter 7 ..... Women And children First................134
Chapter 8 ..... Date With Destiny..........................173
Chapter 9 ..... Mystery Ship.................................192
Chapter 10 ....New York, New York........................221
Conclusion..239

Appreciation...249
Index...250

Prologue

At the same time the pride and flagship of White Star Line, *RMS Titanic* sank to the icy cold bottom of the North Atlantic Ocean at 2.20 am on 15 April 1912, many stories, mostly contradictory of one another started to appear among popular culture in both the U.S. and Britain. Many of the contradicting stories came from the survivors themselves and the popular press of the time.

William Randolph Hearst, who owned the largest newspaper empire in America at the time, ran a series of scathing reports blaming White Star Line. In particular, the managing director, J Bruce Ismay for the disaster, which claimed the lives of 1,512 people, including numerous well-known and influential personalities of American society. By 1919, Hearst was becoming well known for his style of 'Yellow Journalism,' which included: inventing sensational stories, faking and distorting interviews, relaying news stories from the U.K. and Europe, then attributing them to non-existent U.K. and European news correspondents.

The Edwardian era in the United Kingdom was in full swing by 1912. Although King Edward VII had already died in 1910, U.K. society was enjoying great economic and social change, resulting from rapid industrialisation, Society was enjoying more freedoms and independence. In accordance with these changes, fashion faced rapid developments. As the upper classes pursued leisure sports, demanding more mobile and flexible clothing styles. The Edwardian era is known to have been the last time that women wore corsets in everyday life. The British Edwardian era also triggered change in Europe. This was also the time of the French 'Belle Époque,' where Art Nouveau was becoming dominant in architecture. The developments of the automobile and electricity, was influencing the arts, along with a greater awareness of human rights.

Literature was producing great names, such as H. G. Wells, Beatrix Potter, P. G. Wodehouse, Rudyard Kipling and George Bernard Shaw. Mass audience newspapers were becoming critically important in order to keep up to date with fashions and art.

The British Edwardian era was a time of great social divide. The wealthy could buy influence and power in the political arena and the military, increasing their standing in social circles, while the poor remained very poor. This triggered a rise of interest in Socialism to combat the plight of the poor and the lower status of women. In 1893, women were granted the right to vote in New Zealand, followed by South Australia in 1895. The Women's suffrage movement was increasing in popularity in the United Kingdom, Europe and the United States.

The Edwardian era was also a time of innocence. Although the notion of innocence of the era persists into the twenty first century, that innocence was lost when *RMS Titanic* sank beneath the icy cold, frigid North Atlantic Ocean. Many legends and myths grew up among the actual events leading up to how and why an ocean liner the size and luxury of *Titanic* could simply sink after colliding with an iceberg. Stories surfaced that she sank in one piece. Others say she broke apart just prior to sinking. Many claim the iceberg created a massive gash in her bow, allowing her to sink in just under three hours, when her designers and builders claimed she was practically unsinkable. That term "practically" was somehow lost in translation soon after the disaster.

A curse from an Egyptian mummy has been blamed for the sinking, as were many other supposed causes, such as a German U-Boat, used in a vain attempt to trigger World War I, through to the navigation of the ship being taken from the Captain by the ship's owners, in an attempt to win the prestigious Blue Riband, for the fastest trans-Atlantic crossing.

Many stories surfaced claiming *Titanic* did not sink. It was actually her sister ship, *Olympic* in a wrangle over insurance claims, after *Olympic* was involved in a collision with a Royal Navy cruiser.

The managing director and chairman of White Star line, J Bruce Ismay, was branded a coward in the United States, but returned home to Liverpool a hero, until the rumours from the U. S. caught up with him in another inquiry into the sinking.

Titanic's Captain, Edward J. Smith was initially honoured as a hero. But individual eyewitness survivors claim contradicting stories. These eyewitness accounts of events have been lost over time and forgotten. Including the claim that First Officer William Murdoch shot himself, while trying to oversee the launching of the lifeboats in an orderly manner.

According to the eyewitness testimony, a high ranking officer did shoot himself, but that high ranking officer was not Murdoch, but another officer who has gone down in history as a hero, while going down with his ship.

Many of the myths surrounding the *Titanic* story were discounted and many questions answered when the wreck site was discovered on September 1, 1985. However, the persistence of stories that have been retold over the generations have continued to cloud over what really happened, causing the *Titanic* story to continue to be a legend, full of myths and folklore.

Titanic the Legend, Myths and Folklore, unravels those stories that, overtime have become part of the legend, and presents the actual accounts of the Titanic disaster, while pointing out the myths and folklore that persist in literature written since 1912, and the movies that insist on including the myths to present a more interesting story that is, **Titanic**.

Introduction

Science and technology advanced in great leaps in the United Kingdom over Queen Victoria's nearly 64-year reign, from May 24, 1819 to January 22, 1901. Her death ushered in the Edwardian Period.

The Edwardian Period or the "Gilded Age" as it was known as an age that attracted millions of immigrants from Europe. It is also known as a time where there were great leaps and strides in technology, a period of widespread economic growth in the United States. As well as a great gap between the social classes of society. The rich were extremely rich; living like royalty in unrivalled opulence.

While the rich were flaunting their wealth in glamorous social circles, the poor were extremely poor, living in unimaginable poverty and wretched conditions, working in industries and factories for very little pay and poor working conditions. The middle class in this mix were generally made up of Doctors, School Teachers and professionals neither living in poverty nor wealth. Though, the middle class did make a good living and stood a good chance of attaining power and wealth.

This great leap forward in the American economy attracted millions of European migrants, sparking an explosion in ocean travel between Europe and the United States. Both rich and poor were travelling on the increasing number of vessels crossing the Atlantic. For the rich, it meant a business trip or a vacation. For the poor it meant a new way of life in the New World, a brighter future in the "land of opportunity".

In the early years of this great mass migration, conditions onboard these trans-Atlantic vessels were dreadful for both the rich and poor. Before the advent of iron hulled ships, the cabins for the rich were small. The First class passengers were often tossed around, making the task of getting dressed difficult and could often result in injury. For the steerage passengers in the bowels of the ships, the conditions were unimaginable.

Being cramped together in the bowels of the ship with minimal ventilation. Sanitation and comfort were unheard of. The U.S. Immigration laws prohibited them access to the fresh air on deck.

However, the industrial revolution helped improve ship-building techniques and the invention of steam-power, together with iron-hulled vessels allowed for much larger ships, which, in turn, led to greater stability and comfort.

As onboard accommodation became larger, ships provided larger areas for all passengers, so that, by the time Titanic was built, steerage-class passengers had their own cabins and communal mess-halls for meals and entertainment.

Meanwhile, the British Cunard Line had been virtually unchallenged in ferrying migrants on the trans-Atlantic run well into the 1800's. In 1867, Thomas Henry Ismay bought the White Star Line, which was founded in 1850 and was mainly centred on trade to the Australian gold mines. In 1889 Ismay founded the Oceanic Steam Navigation Company in an attempt to establish White Star Line into the lucrative Atlantic passenger trade. White Star finally found itself the leader in the trans-Atlantic trade after building its sixth ship, *Baltic* and setting the East Bound Atlantic Speed record four years later and, despite the wreck of *RMS Atlantic* in 1873, the new company continued to rival and eventually surpass Cunard.

The competition for Atlantic supremacy was fierce. Often one company would surpass and dominate, then, another would take advantage of newer technology and overtake the other. In 1889, White Star Line launched *RMS Teutonic* and *RMS Majestic*, ushering in a new era of ocean liner. While their competitors were still using a mix of steam engines and sails. White Star Line's newest vessels had no sails, leaving the decks spacious and uncluttered. Soon size and comfort became paramount in ocean travel. Speed alone was becoming less important. The quality of travel was becoming most important.

This fierce competition and increase in passenger travel caught the eye of American financier John Pierpont Morgan. Morgan immediately started buying up the smaller shipping companies, which were competing with White Star Line and Cunard Line, under a trust called The Mercantile Marine Company. Morgan had gained enormous wealth through both Steel and Railroad industries. The International Mercantile Marine Company could operate easily without returning a profit, for as long as it took to put White Star Line and Cunard Line out of business. So, he immediately cut the cost of third class travel to America, with the goal of gaining control over his two major competitors.

With a competitor such as J.P. Morgan, who was stealing virtually all immigrant passengers, White Star Line and Cunard were facing difficulties. Cunard Line had gained financial support from the British Government, that allowed them to compete with the International Mercantile Marine prices. White Star Line, however, were in trouble.

In 1899, Thomas Henry Ismay died, leaving control of White Star to his son, Joseph Bruce Ismay. Because J Bruce Ismay was far less experienced than his father, White Star faced financial ruin. This was deeply concerning to Lord William Pirrie who ran Harland and Wolff shipyards.

Harland and Wolff was built on reclaimed land that was piled up in Belfast harbour during dredging in the 1840s to allow bigger ships to pass through. Harland and Wolff was originally built by Robert Hickson and Company, who began building iron ships in 1853, Edward J. Harland became manager a year later and took control of the company in 1859. Harland and Wolff was born in 1861 when he joined up with G.W Wolff. William Pirrie began working as an apprentice at the age of 15, in 1862. After rising through the ranks with the shipbuilders, Pirrie became a partner in 1874 at the age of 27. After taking control of the company in 1906, he became Lord William Pirrie.

Harland and Wolff had built all White Star ships since 1869. If White Star failed, this would lose the shipbuilder a major source of business, which was why Pirrie was so concerned. He recommended to Bruce Ismay that he consider selling White Star to the International Mercantile Marine Company, as this would not only save White Star, it would also ensure the future of the growing German shipping companies and Cunard could be destroyed once and for all. Pirrie was also expecting to generate more business for Harland and Wolff in the process. In 1902, Ismay sold White Star to IMM and JP Morgan kept Ismay on as Managing Director. Morgan also gave Ismay and Pirrie complete autonomy, telling them to spare no expense in building the best ship.

We have arrived at a new time. Let us realise it. And with that new time strange methods, huge forces, large combinations - a Titanic world - have sprung up around us.

—Winston Churchill, 23 May. 1909

CHAPTER ONE

The Dream Is Born

*R**M.S. Titanic* was the second of three Olympic-class ocean liners owned by the International Mercantile Marine Company, and operated by the White Star Line on the Trans-Atlantic passenger route, between Southampton and New York City. At her time of launch, on 31 May 1911, she was the largest ship afloat and was unparalleled for comfort and luxury. *Titanic* was slightly larger than her sister, *RMS Olympic,* which was launched the previous year and entered service with her maiden voyage on 14 June 1911. *Titanic* dwarfed *Olympic* in volume and weight. Her total weight was 46,328 gross registered tons, compared to *Olympic's* 45,324 gross registered tons. Making *Titanic,* the heaviest and finest ship afloat.

At the beginning of the 20th Century, intense competition existed between shipping lines, in particular the White Star Line and Cunard Line. Cunard were a formidable competitor with two standout ships belonging to their fleet, the *RMS Lusitania* and *RMS Mauretania*, which were ranked as the top in sophistication and luxury on the lucrative Trans-Atlantic route between Liverpool and New York. Cunard's *RMS Mauretania* entered service in 1907, at 790 feet long, weighing 30,000 tons. Cunard's two new ships were the talk of the shipping industry and immediately set the standard of travel that White Star dreamed of replicating. *Mauretania* immediately set a speed record for the fastest Trans-Atlantic crossing, with speeds in excess of 26 knots. *RMS Mauretania* held the record for 22 years. *RMS Lusitania* entered service the same year and was heralded for its opulence and spectacular interior.

In the summer of the same year, J. Bruce Ismay, the chairman and Chief executive of White Star Line, met with Lord William James Pirrie, chairman and chief executive of Belfast based Harland and Wolff ship builders, at Downshire House - Pirrie's London home, to discuss the construction of three new vessels. The three new White Star vessels would permanently alter the history of human travel and outclass the two new Cunard Line vessels in standard of travel and comfort. The ships would be 50% larger than *Lusitania* and *Mauritania*, although not as fast.

The new Olympic-class vessels would surpass all other ships ever built in sheer size and luxury. The first liner, *Olympic* would set the standard in ocean travel and her sisters *Titanic* and *Britannic*, would indeed surpass that standard. The trio were to be the largest moving objects ever built by man and would put White Star at the forefront of the race to dominate the shipping routes of the North Atlantic.

Ismay and Pirrie very quickly put into motion the events that would lead to the creation of the three super liners, that summer evening in London. Pirrie's nephew, Thomas Andrews, a brilliant young engineer and dedicated Naval Architect, would be placed in charge of the overall design of the three vessels.

Thomas Andrews was barely 40 years old when he was appointed chief designer for the Olympic-Class liners at Harland and Wolff. He was responsible for producing every drawing of every part of the ships and he would later travel on *Titanic's* maiden voyage. Continually writing down notes in a book he always carried around, Andrews used the notes to provide alterations, suggestions on improvements for *Titanic* and the construction of the third Olympic-Class vessel, *Britannic*, thus ensuring they would become the most magnificent vessels and super-liners of ocean-going luxury of their time.

In addition to Andrew's keen supervision of the design process. Ismay also played an active role - insisting on being consulted on any changes to the design. Andrews was the managing director of the design department. But, Ismay had the final say on all decisions regarding the development of the Olympic-class liners.

Ismay noted that the Cunard vessels had four funnels on their ships and envisioned the new White Star liners would have three funnels and four masts. Pirrie altered the design to add an extra funnel, which would simply serve as ventilation for the engine room. Pirrie reasoned that four funnels would provide a more commanding presence for the White Star Line ships and raking the funnels backwards would provide the impression of speed, even when the ships were stationary.

Pirrie also altered the number of masts from Ismay's four to two, one forward and the other aft of the four funnels. Reasoning, any more would make the new ships appear to be sailing ships.

Harland and Wolff drew up a contract with the White Star Line, providing the three new ships on a "Cost Plus" agreement basis. This meant that, no matter how much the cost of building the ships increased during the construction period, the shipbuilder was guaranteed to make a profit on the agreement. The average profit margin in contracts such as this was 5%, often being paid for in share stock in the contracting company.

The new Olympic-Class vessels would be 882 feet long and 92.5 feet wide at their widest point, making them the largest vessels afloat at that time. Construction of *R.M.S. Titanic* was funded by the American, J. P. Morgan and the International Mercantile Marine Co.

In early 1908, the designs were finished and by the end of March an order for the three new ships was officially placed with Harland and Wolff. As soon as the construction on the new gantries was completed, White

Star Line's Olympic- class super liners could become reality. A dream would be born.

The Construction

This was definitely a new age, a new Era. The world had never seen anything like *Olympic* and, especially the newer, *Titanic*. No moving objects, the size of these mammoths, had ever been constructed by man. From the start of construction, it was with pride from the lowest worker to the highest management of Harland and Wolff that such a vision could be conceived from its embryonic stages. Then, grow to dominate the world of ocean travel.

At the time of their construction, 15,000 people worked at Harland and Wolff. To accommodate the new ships' construction, Harland and Wolff were faced with a major engineering problem. No shipbuilding yard had faced the challenges associated with attempting to build ships the size of the Olympic-Class vessels. The ships were constructed on Queens Island in Belfast Harbour, now known as, Titanic Quarter. The slipways had to be re-engineered for their enormous weight and size. To accommodate them, three previous slipways had to be demolished. The vessels' enormous size posed some extra problems. A gantry was constructed over slipways 2 and 3 that could accommodate both ships. The giant gantry measured 840 feet long by 240 feet wide and 228 feet high to the top of the upper crane. It was equipped with four large electric lifts and a system of cranes. A separate crane, capable of lifting 200 tons had to be brought in from Germany.

The giant gantry housing the hull of Titanic

The layout of the slipways and gantry enabled the construction of both *Olympic* and *Titanic* to take place virtually side by side. Both ships were built following similar construction methods. Construction consisted of a Keel backbone with 300 ribs consisting of the frame, 24 inches and 36 inches apart and 66 feet high, measured from the Keel to the ships Bridge deck. It was decided that the ships would not utilise the double skin hull that had been used in previous vessels, but would, instead, utilise the double bottom design, extending all the way up the side of the hull. The double bottom, the outer hull and the inner hull was about 5 feet 3 inches apart and utilised 2,000 steel plates to form the outer skin of the hull. The sheets were exceptionally heavy, but as speed was not a consideration or a factor in the design, this did not matter. The exceptional weight of the steel plates, were deemed necessary for the strength required for such mammoth vessels.

The 2,000 plates were single sheets of rolled steel, up to 6 feet or 1.8 m wide and 30 feet or 9.1m long, weighing roughly 2.5 to 3 tons each, varying in thickness 1.5 inches or 3.8 cm to 1 inch or 2.5 cm thick. The plates were laid in a layered or clinkered fashion from Keel to bilge. Above the ships' bilge, the plates were laid out in the in and out or strake plating fashion, where the plates are overlapped, then riveted together. Using over three million iron and steel rivets, which, them selves weighed 1,200 tons. The rivets were mostly fitted by hydraulic machines and by hammering by hand in areas the hydraulic machines could not reach. The hull of *Titanic* had over 2000 portholes for the wealthier passengers to view the sea rolling past the ship.

Worker Trapped in Titanic Hull

Was a shipyard worker at Harland and Wolff trapped inside the *Titanic's* double bottom hull? Rumour during the ships construction certainly claims there was. Work was progressing on her construction so well that the rumour grew.

Titanic is not the only occasion in human history where a worker is supposed to have been trapped during construction. Such myths grew over time as construction methods and speed increased. The Egyptian pyramids certainly have their share of workers suddenly finding themselves trapped inside as the buildings rapidly grew around them, especially as these structures became more important than the men creating them. The 20th century also has such tales. The Hoover Dam for instance where, one or more workers did find themselves entombed forever - with all the activity going on around them, no one noticed they were missing.

Titanic is not unique with such stories around shipbuilding. In 1859, *The Great Eastern* was constructed. *The Great Eastern* was a true giant of a ship, six times larger than any other ship at that time. Rumours were rife of a worker trapped in her double hull throughout her life. Eventually, when she was scrapped 30 years later, reports surfaced, claiming the skeleton of a worker was discovered in her hull. However, no documented evidence has ever surfaced to support the claim.

In reality, injuries and deaths, resulting from accidents were surprisingly rare during *Titanic's* construction. The standard notion at the time was, shipbuilding yards should expect a ratio of one worker death per £100.000 spent. On that basis, *Titanic* should have had dozens of deaths during her construction. In fact, only eight deaths were verified between her Keel laying, until her launch. Her 'construction to death' ratio was regarded as an incredible achievement. In fact, every worker involved in the construction of *Titanic* was accounted for at the end of every day.

The origins of the 'entombed worker' myth are quite understandable and certainly not surprising. At the end of the working day at Harland and Wolff, inspectors would check the quality of the rivets by tapping on them with a hammer, to calculate the pay for the riveters. It's not surprising that the sound made by the inspectors would have led some older workers to explain to gullible, younger workers, the tapping sound was from a trapped worker who was hoping to be freed from the hull. The same myth also mentions, some passengers onboard *Titanic* heard the tapping from the ghost of the trapped worker. These stories have never been verified

~~ ~~ ~~ ~~

Lord Pirrie watched with great pride as the first of the three super liners, *Olympic* arose from the ground up. The first ship with the gigantic gantry that would, propel Harland and Wolff to the forefront of shipbuilding, using the innovative technology and building method the rest of the world would strive to equal.

Work on the new Olympic-Class liners began with the keel of *R.M.S. Olympic* being laid on 16 December 1908, on slipway 2, followed by her sister ship, *Titanic* on 31 March 1909, on slipway 3. *Olympic* was launched on 20 October 1911, watched by a massive crowd of 18.000 people. A tradition with White Star Line and Harland and Wolff was that the first ship built in a class would be painted all white, with a black line between Deck D and C, separating the hull from the superstructure.

Titanic was not alone in the massive gantry for long - the Keel of *Britannic* was laid soon after *Olympic's* launch. Work continued non-stop on *Titanic* at a frantic pace until her launch on 31 May 1911.

390904 = No Pope

After *Titanic* sank, claims were made of a curse, known as the Titanic Curse, linked to the White Star Lines practice of never christening their ships when launched. Another was suggested with the ships hull number, being 390904 spelled out NOPOPE when reflected on a mirror. This 'NOPOPE' slogan was believed to be a direct attack on the Roman Catholic faith. Harland and Wolff are situated in East Belfast, Northern Ireland. The Northern Ireland region has a large sectarian, Protestant population. Thus, *Titanic's* sinking was believed by some to have been as a result of anti-Catholic sentiment held by the ships builders.

Harland and Wolff were known for hiring few Catholics, though it is unclear whether this was a result of anti-catholic sentiment, or the area of East Belfast being mainly a protestant area to which few Catholics would travel, so few Catholics would work.

The 'No Pope' Myth of the *Titanic* tragedy implies that Catholic workers at Harland and Wolff noticed the blasphemous message, possibly by the numbers being reflected into a puddle of water or by looking into a mirror and seeing the supposed anti-catholic slogan. As is the case with mythology, it is not clear how the slogan was first noticed. However, what is known is that the Catholic workforce refused to work, until management explained that the 'NOPOPE' message was purely coincidental. As the story of the hull number spread throughout Ireland, many people took the view that Harland and Wolff was a hotbed of anti-Catholic sentiment. Other stories also soon spread of how Catholics were treated at Harland and Wolff. The stories also served to illustrate the attitudes of many Catholics towards the Protestant population!

In fact, the CEO of Harland and Wolff, Lord Pirrie, was sympathetic toward Catholics and refused to allow such nonsense of antagonism between Protestants and Catholic to exist at Harland and Wolff. There never existed any employment policy that barred Catholics from working at their yards, or unfair treatment towards Roman Catholics.

For the 'No Pope' myth to be true, The Hull number of 390904 would have to be true. Actually, the number of 390904 was never assigned to *Titanic*, as a hull number or another number. *Titanic's* actual Hull number was 131428 - her Build Number or official Board of Trade designation. The shipyard number assigned to *Titanic* was 401. As, *Titanic* was the four hundred and first ship built at Harland and Wolff. Her slipway number was No 3.

As stated earlier, it is not exactly clear where the myth of the number 390904 originated. Certainly not long after the ship sank, many people were asking just how a ship built from iron and steel, a triumph of modern technology and pride, could sink after a collision with an iceberg, which is only frozen water. Surely the disaster could not be the result of an accident. Some came to believe the sinking was obviously an act of divine retribution. This view was particularly strong among the Southern Irish Roman Catholics.

Northern Ireland, in particular, Belfast, where Harland and Wolff is located, has a mainly Ulster Protestant population. Antagonism has cursed the relationship between Catholics and Protestants in Ireland for over four hundred years. At the end of the 19th century and the start of the 20th century, the division between Ulster and the rest of Ireland began to take on political overtones. Politics and Religion can create a volatile mix.

As a result of this mix of politics and religion, expressions of defiance grew and the story of the number 390904 gained traction.

That the story of *RMS Titanic* sinking was an Act of divine retribution, because her existence defied the existence of God and denied the existence of the Pope and the Holy church also spread to the Irish communities in the United States. The proof? Well, that was the anti-Catholic message hidden in the ships hull.

~ ~ ~ ~

Many employment and working regulations, concerning safety of workers that are taken for granted in the 21st Century did not exist at the start of the 20th Century. For the 15,000 people who worked on *Titanic*, the work was difficult, and dangerous, safety was rudimentary at best. Most of the work was carried out without safety equipment, such as hard hats or safety guards on machinery. As a result, death or injury, resulting from accidents were expected. 246 injuries were reported during her construction, 28 of those were recorded as severe, for example: Legs crushed by falling sheets of iron and arms severed. Six people were killed on the ship during her construction and fitting out. Two others were killed in the shipyards sheds and workshops. One more was killed after a plank of wood fell on him during the ship's launch.

The two new Cunard ships were dominating the North Atlantic. White Star Line needed to get their new super-liners into service as soon as possible. Since her launch, *Olympic* had undergone seven months outfitting. After two days of sea trials, she was handed over to White Star Line on May 31, 1911. The same day *Titanic's* completed hull was launched.

CHAPTER TWO

Launch

The Titanic was the last word in shipbuilding. Every British regulation had been complied with and her masters, officers and crew were the most experienced and skillful in the British service

- J. Bruce Ismay, chairman and chief executive, White Star Line.

The beginning of the 20th century, Belfast was experiencing its boom years. The city had become the global leader in engineering and linen manufacture. Harland and Wolff had become the largest shipbuilders in the world.

The days leading up to the 31st May 1911, continued to be a hive of activity at the Harland and Wolff shipyards, in preparation for the momentous occasion. The launch day was a celebration for those who worked on her, the shipyard that built her and the shipping line who owned her.

Grandstands were constructed for the thousands of dignitaries, invited ticket holding guests and members of the press who would be present to witness the 26,000 tons of hull, which will eventually belong to the heaviest object ever moved by man, slide into the water of the Queens Island, Belfast Lough. Workers were busy applying 22 tons of tallow - train oil and soap to lubricate the 772 feet or 237 m slipway with a one inch thick layering for *Titanic's* giant three tons per square inch hull to slip down the 'way.

At the time of her launch, the construction was far from complete. *Titanic* was just a massive hull, containing the massive engines, boilers and bulkheads.

- Bulkheads: The 16 watertight compartments of *Titanic* had doors that could close automatically if water rose beyond a certain level, or, could be closed manually by a lever system. Another, third, method was by way of an over ride switch on the ship's bridge using hydraulic cataract cylinders. Ensuring all 15 watertight doors to close within 25 - 30 seconds in the event of an emergency, which could threaten the safety of the ship. By its design, *Titanic* could stay afloat if any two out of four compartments flooded, or she could stay afloat even if any combination of 3 or four compartments flooded.

- Engines: *Titanic's* power source was primarily from triple-expansion reciprocating steam engines, driving her one port and one starboard propellers. The centre propeller was powered by a Parsons low-pressure turbine engine, which gained its power from the two reciprocating engines. The same combination of engines used on the Olympic-class vessels were the same used by the White Star Lines' *RMS Laurentic* with great success. The reciprocating engines ran at 75 rpm and generated 30,000 horsepower. The centre turbine engine ran at 165 rpm and generated 16,000 horsepower. Generating a top speed of 23 to 24 knots.

- Boilers: To power the worlds largest ships during the early 1900's, required an enormous power source for its driving engines. In 1912, the source of the power was provided by coal powered steam. *Titanic* had twenty-four double ended Scotch class boilers and a further five single ended boilers, housed in six boiler rooms. The double ended boilers measured 20 feet long with a diameter of fifteen feet, nine inches and contained six coal burning furnaces. The ship was fitted with 29 boilers and 159 furnaces.

Over 8,000 tons of coal filled her bunkers. The fired furnaces heated water in the boilers to generate steam at 215 psi, then funneling steam to the triple-expansion engines, generating the energy required to turn the propellers. All boilers generating 46,000 horsepower.

Much more work would still be required for construction of her superstructure and fitting out. Then a series of sea trials will have to be executed, before she could be declared seaworthy for passenger and cargo on the Trans-Atlantic service.

Early in the morning of the 31st May 1911, the ships workers, their families, casual observers, important guests, members of the press and others who wished to witness history in the making, began to arrive at Harland and Wolff. It was estimated that around 100,000 people - about one third of the total population of Belfast would arrive to watch *Titanic* slip from the cradle of her birth into the water. The Crimson, Blue and White grandstands had been decorated with banners displaying the American Stars and Stripes, The British Red Ensign and the White Star Line logo. The giant Arrol Gantry that had previously encased the hull of *Olympic* and the newer, ready to be launched *Titanic* was also decorated with the British Red Ensign and the American Stars and Stripes gallantly flying at its highest point, while signal flags spelled out the words "Good Luck".

Lord Pirie (left) and J. Bruce Ismay (right)

During the buildup to the launching ceremony, Harland and Wolff's Chief Executive and Chairman Lord Pirrie and White Star Line's Chief Executive and Chairman J. Bruce Ismay made a tour of inspection of *Titanic's* hull.

J.P. Morgan, Bruce Ismay, his daughter Margaret, Lord and Lady Pirrie, Thomas Andrews, the Lord Mayor of Belfast, Dignitaries, invited guests and the press occupied the grandstands at the slipway. In front of them, the 26,000 ton hull of *Titanic*. The workers, their families and others who wished to witness this monumental occasion had to make do with any vantage point they could find.

Just before mid day, two red rockets climbed high into the sky over the shipyard, announcing to the amassed crowd that the launch was imminent and signaling for the huge supporting beams to be knocked free from under the leviathan. The last death of a workman to be killed during *Titanic's* construction occurred at this point, as a large supporting timber fell on James Dobbins, who received serious injuries. Dobbins died from his injuries later that day in a local Belfast hospital.

There was no christening for *Titanic,* as there was also none for her sister, *Olympic*. White Star Line vessels were not christened with the traditional bottle of Champagne smashed against the Bow, in line with White Star Line company policy.

At 12.13pm on May 31, 1911, a third red rocket was fired high into the sky. This third and last rocket signaled the order to release the hydraulic launch triggers that held the monstrous hull in place on the slipway. The largest movable object created by man was moving under her own weight for the first time.

Titanic took 62 seconds to slide down the slipway and into the water. In that time, she had travelled nearly twice her length at a speed of 12 knots, before being brought to a halt in the river Lagan, by six anchor chains and two piles of drag chains, weighing 80 tons each.

Bruce Ismay and other guests of Lord Pirrie, went to the Queens Island yard for an expensive lunch. At 3.00pm, Ismay and his party boarded *Titanic's* completed sister, *Olympic* for her first sailing, Southampton.

The freshly launched hull was towed by tugs from Liverpool's Alexander Towing Company, using the tugs, *Alexander*, *Hornby*, *Herculaneum* and *Wallasey* and assisted by Harland and Wolff's own tug, *Hercules*, to her fitting out basin for the next phase of her construction.

The Fitting Out

Soon after *Titanic's* launch was completed, she was moved to the Harland and Wolff fitting out basin, where the empty shell of the vessel would be turned into the incredible floating palace she would become renowned for being. The builders who constructed her impressive hull were now concentrating on completing the third hull of the Olympic-class trio, that of *Britannic*.

Now securely placed in the fitting out basin of the deep water wharf of Harland and Wolff, It was now the turn of the highly skilled craftsmen to create her lavish interiors. An army of Joiners, Plumbers, Tilers, Carpet Layers, Electricians, Steamfitters, Metalworkers and Painters, worked tirelessly to build her superstructure, install her four funnels and create her legendary cabins and rooms. Hundreds and thousands of items kept arriving by ship, train and road at Harland and Wolff for *Titanic's* fitting.

Many of the manufacturers who were supplying goods for *Titanic* made sure their customers and potential customers knew about it. Many advertising materials began to display images of *Titanic*, along with the product name. After all, what better endorsement or promotion, than to be able to announce that your product is being placed on the finest ship in the world, to be used by the most famous and wealthy people in the world?

Some alterations were made during *Titanic's* fitting out, that differentiated her from her older sister, *Olympic*. For example, some passengers on *Olympic* had complained to White Star Line that spray from the ocean was making them wet as they strolled along the forward section of the promenade deck. The spray was coming up from the bow of the ship. Bruce Ismay ordered the area to be installed with sliding glass panels to protect the passengers from spray, although the panels could be opened. This feature of *Titanic* is quite striking from her sister, *RMS Olympic* as she retained the open forward section of her promenade deck. This feature of *Titanic* also made her easier to identify from a distance.

The superstructure consisted of two decks, the Promenade Deck and Boat Deck, which were about 500 feet or 150 m long. They accommodated the officers' quarters, gymnasium, public rooms and first-class cabins, plus the bridge and wheelhouse. The ships' lifeboats were carried on the Boat Deck, the uppermost deck. Standing above the decks were four funnels, though only three were functional. The last being a dummy, installed for aesthetic purposes, two masts, one forward, one aft of the funnels, each 155 feet or 47 m high, which supported derricks for loading cargo. A wireless aerial was slung between the masts.

Big Gash in the side of Titanic

Conflicting testimony from the 700 survivors and stories included in hundreds of books for 85 years out of over the last 100 years since the *Titanic* disaster, indicated a giant gash along 300 feet out of the 900 feet length of the vessels starboard side, inflicted from the collision with the iceberg, allowing the massive ship to sink in two and a half hours, with the loss of over 1500 victims.

How was it possible for a ship so costly and exceptionally well built for safety and luxury to sink so fast after a mere collision with an iceberg? The ship was designed to survive the flooding of three or four of her watertight compartments, depending on which variation of four compartments.

In the 1912, British Board Of Trade inquiry into the sinking of *Titanic*, Harland and Wolff Naval architect Edward Wilding, suggested that the uneven flooding of the watertight compartments meant she had suffered unique, non-continuous damage. Wilding further suggested that the damage might be relatively small. But Wilding's testimony was widely ignored, because of the general belief that the only damage that could possibly have sunk such a vessel would have been the massive gash along *Titanic's* side.

Many questions and myths relating to *Titanic* were laid to rest after the 1985 discovery of *Titanic's* resting place, by Dr Robert Ballard of the Woods Hole Oceanographic Institution and iFremer. The biggest discovery was that the ship actually did break apart as she sank. The discovery opened up more questions, including the question of the size of the damage that caused the ship to sink. The myth of the gash was re-enforced, for a short time, in 1992, in Dr Robert MacInnis' published book, "*Titanic in a new light*". MacInnis suggested that repeated strikes to brittle plates could have caused them to disintegrate, one after the other. Or, in effect, opening up the starboard side of the ship.

In August 1996, further dives onto the wreck by French state oceanographic group, iFremer, finally set the myth to rest. Using images created by ultra-sound to examine the Starboard hull, as the damaged area is hidden under up to 55 feet of mud.

Examining the hull of *Titanic*, in a similar way, a doctor examines a pregnant woman, the president of Polaris Imaging Incorporated, Paul K. Matthias with a 26 foot French submersible, discovered a series of deformations of six thin openings, no larger than a persons hand, that start and stop, along the hull, about hand, that start and stop, along the hull, about 10 feet above the bottom of the ship. Matthias said:

"They appear to follow the ships plate" suggesting that iron rivets along the plate seams probably popped open to create splits. Matthias observed the longest gap was 36 feet long, extending between boiler rooms No 5 and No 6, crossing between the watertight bulkhead.

The gaps in the plates are small. But the pressure from the ocean outside, would have forced the water through, in much the same way, as would jets of water from a fireman's hose, filling the interior of the ship with thirty nine thousand tons of water just before she sank.

~ ~ ~ ~

During the summer of 1911, Bruce Ismay proposed the maiden voyage of *Titanic* would take place on March 20, 1912. White Star Line began issuing timetables, posters and stationary advertising the March 1912 sailing date. However, events soon began to conspire to postpone this date. One such event was that *RMS Olympic* was involved in a collision with the Royal Navy cruiser, *HMS Hawke*, canceling *Olympic's* fifth voyage, under the command of Captain E.J. Smith. Although no one was injured and the ship stayed afloat, the damage was severe enough to warrant immediate repairs. Work on *Titanic* stopped while repairs were made to *Olympic's* hull, as Harland and Wolff were the only company to have a dry dock large enough to cater for these large vessels. Workers attached to *Titanic* were transferred to *Olympic*, which meant that the timetable for the maiden voyage of *Titanic* had to be re-arranged. Another date was issued by White Star Line in London for April 10, 1912.

The repair work on *RMS Olympic* was completed on November 30th, 1911. *Olympic* returned to Southampton to once again begin and complete her fifth voyage to New York and the fitting out of *Titanic* resumed.

The fitting of *Titanic's* machinery, heavy equipment and the installation of her majestic interiors took ten months and several million man-hours. More luxurious than her predecessor, her fitting out was intended to make her the most impressive vessel the world had ever seen. Between teak from Siam, fabrics from Holland, thick carpeting, where one worker commented "so thick, you sank in it up to your knees." One prestigious industry journal stated "The greatest pains were being taken to provide passenger accommodations of unrivaled extent and magnificence… The excellent result defies improvement".

Already a thousand tons heavier than *Olympic*, *Titanic* sported many design refinements that made her far more luxurious than her sister. Her first class restaurant was enlarged and included a trellised replica of a French sidewalk café, The Café Parisian. Two first class suites were built on B. Deck. These staterooms had private promenades, which required alterations to be made to the B. Deck window arrangements, as well as the alterations to the open section on A. Deck, or the Promenade deck, which were installed to eliminate the annoying sea spray that some *Olympic* passengers had complained about.

Titanic (left) Displaying the enclosed Promenade deck (A. Deck) and Olympic (right). Promenade deck is open. Just below the boat deck

Upon completion, *Titanic* featured ten decks. Below the Boat Deck were decks A, B, C, D, E, F and G deck. Below G. Deck were the Boiler Rooms and Holds. Below them was the Orlop Deck. The fifteen watertight Bulkheads, extended to F. Deck.

- The Boat Deck - The uppermost deck, excluding the top of the Officers quarters is the deck the lifeboats were situated. The bridge stood eight feet or 2.4 m above the forward end, extending out both sides, so the ship could be controlled while docking. The wheelhouse was slightly above and immediately behind the bridge, with the officers and Captains quarters directly behind the wheelhouse. Situated at mid-ships was the entrance to the First Class Grand Staircase and the gymnasium along with the raised roof of the First Class lounge. Towards the aft of the boat deck was the roof of the first class smoke room and modest Second class entrance. The wood-carved deck was divided into four segregated promenades: For officers, First class passengers, engineers and Second class passengers respectively. Lifeboats lined the forward and aft of the deck, excluding the First class areas at mid-ships, so the view would not be spoilt.

- A Deck - Also known as the promenade Deck, extended the full length of the superstructure. The promenade deck was reserved for First class passengers and contained cabins, the First class lounge, smoking room, reading and writing rooms and the Verandah Cafe, also known as Palm Court.

- B Deck - Or the Bridge Deck, the top weight-bearing deck and the uppermost level of the hull. On this deck were six palatial First class staterooms, each featuring its own private promenade. Unlike the *Olympic*, *Titanic's* B Deck also contained the A La Carte restaurant and the Café Parisian providing luxury dining for First class passengers. Also located on this deck was the Second class smoking room and entrance hall. B Deck also contained a raised forecastle containing number 1 hatch, this being the main hatch through to the cargo holds, various pieces of machinery and the Anchor housing. At the rear of this deck was the raised poop deck, 106 feet or 32m long, the poop deck was used as a promenade for Third class passengers.

- C. Deck - The Shelter Deck. The highest deck to run completely from Bow to Stern. The Third class promenade and the Third class cabins and public rooms were contained at the aft end of the poop deck. The majority of First class cabins and Second class library were situated midships, with the crew's cabins being situated under the forecastle deck.

- D. Deck - The Saloon Deck. The highest deck reached by eight of the fifteen watertight bulkheads. The Saloon Deck was dominated by three large public rooms - the First Class Reception Room and Dining Room. The Second Class Dining Room, plus an open area for Third Class passengers. First, Second and Third Class passengers had cabins on this deck. The firemen's cabins were located in the Bow.

- E. Deck - The Upper Deck, was predominantly used for accommodation for First, Second and Third Class passengers, plus Berths for Cooks, Seamen, Stewards and Trimmers. A long passageway, nicknamed 'Scotland Road' - named after a famous road in Liverpool, ran along its length. 'Scotland Road' was used by Third Class passengers and crew members.

- F. Deck - The Middle Deck. The swimming pool and Turkish bath were situated on this deck. Second and Third Class passengers were mainly accommodated, together with several departments for the crew as well as the Third Class Dining saloon.

- G. Deck - The Lower Deck. The lowest complete deck that carried passengers. Just above the waterline, G deck had the lowest portholes. The Squash Courts and the traveling Post Office were located here, where mail clerks sorted letters and parcels so they would be ready for delivery when the ship docked and food was also stored on this deck. The deck was interrupted at several points by Orlop or partial decks over the boiler, engine and turbine rooms.

- Orlop Deck and Tank Top - The lowest level below the waterline, is where cargo was stowed. The Tank Top was the inner bottom of the ships hull - providing the platform on which the boilers, engines, turbines and electrical generators were positioned. This area was dominated by the engine and boiler rooms and was 'off limits' to passengers. The deck was connected with the higher levels by flights of stairs and twin spiral stairways located near the bow to access D Deck.

Titanic was equipped with four 400 kilowatt generators, providing First and Second class passenger comforts which equaled that of the top Hotels of Europe and America. All cabins had electric lighting and heaters. First Class enjoyed features such as an electric camel in the gymnasium and a heated swimming pool.

An electric elevator took First and Second Class passengers between decks. Steerage accommodation and facilities were exceptionally good for the time. Many of the Third Class passengers would never have enjoyed electric lighting and heating before they boarded *Titanic*. The generators also powered the loading cranes, cooking in the galley, refrigerating the huge stores of fresh food down on the Orlop Deck, lighting and heating the public areas, the ventilation fans, operating the watertight doors, the telephone system and the Marconi wireless equipment.

Unsinkable.

The myth that *Titanic* was unsinkable is by far the most popular in literature written about the disaster and in the scripts of *Titanic* movies over the last century. The 1997 James Cameron movie "*Titanic*" depicts this myth as a popular belief in 1912. At the beginning of the movie, while arriving at the White Star Line wharf at Southampton, prior to boarding, the character of Ruth DeWitt Bukater, when looking at the massive ship in front of her comments:

"So this is the ship they say is unsinkable" to which the character of Cal Hockley replies: "It is unsinkable. Not even god himself could sink this ship".

The character of Cal Hockley, seems to be stating this myth to be fact. In reality, before *Titanic's* maiden voyage, and certainly before her tragic accident with the iceberg, and subsequent sinking, nobody thought *Titanic* was unsinkable. The second sentence from Cal Hockley is also not true. His statement " Not even god himself could sink this ship," is believed to have been a comment from a White Star Line employee. Many versions of the myth claim Captain Smith made the comment, a Steward made the comment, a senior officer made the comment. Some mention an unnamed employee made the comment. Reality is, no one made such a comment.

Titanic, her sister ships *Olympic* and *Britannic*, were designed according to the 1891 Grade 1 subdivision, proposed by the Bulkhead committee, meaning the three Olympic-class vessels could stay afloat with any four of her 16 adjoining compartments below the waterline open to the water. In the case of the Olympic-class vessels, *Olympic* and *Titanic*, the bulkhead height extended to at least E. Deck. This was well above that which was required, so *Titanic* and *Olympic* could stay afloat with any combination of four compartments open to the water, or any combination of four adjoining compartments open to the water, thus making *Titanic* "practically unsinkable".

With the construction of the third liner, *Britannic*, launched on 26 February 1914, this was changed and the bulkhead height extended to B. Deck, as a result of the *Titanic* disaster. Watertight doors also provided thoroughfares between compartments.

Titanic's 15 watertight doors were normally operated vertically on hydraulic cataract cylinders. In an emergency however, the doors could be operated in three different ways. First was by a switch on the bridge, which operated the hydraulic cataract cylinders that ensured that as soon as one door started to close, the others would also close. Alternatively each door could be individually closed by way of either a lever or a float mechanism under the floor, so that if a compartment was flooding, the incoming water would trigger the mechanism and the doors would close. When the watertight doors were closed via any of the three methods, they would close within 25-30 seconds.

Titanic's broadside with an iceberg on the night of April 14, 1912 breached five adjoining forward compartments, nearly 300 feet or 91.4 metres, opening them to the water. This ensured *Titanic* would sink. An unqualified comment was made to the *New York Times* news paper on 16 April 1912, two days after *Titanic's* sinking, by Philip A. S. Franklin, Vice President of the International Mercantile Marine Company, stating:

"I thought her unsinkable, and I based my opinion on the best expert advice available. I do not understand it". After that comment was published, it was seized upon by the media and entered the publics' perception that White Star Line had previously believed that *Titanic* was unsinkable.

Titanic, was never described as "unsinkable" by her operators, White Star Line, or her builders, Harland and Wolff. Three trade publications in which one was never published, described her as "practically unsinkable" prior to the collision with the iceberg. The notion of her being "unsinkable" had not entered the public arena until after her sinking. A promotional item from White Star Line, prior to her maiden voyage claimed;

"As far as it is possible to do so, these two wonderful vessels are designed to be unsinkable."

No one could reasonably imagine the scenario that doomed *Titanic*. There remains a possibility that Philip A. S. Franklin misinterpreted that White Star Line promotional item.

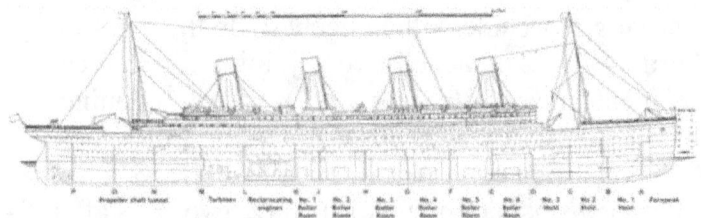

Diagram of Titanic showing Bulkheads (Red), Engineering areas noted (Blue), Name of decks (Right), areas of iceberg damage (Green)

~ ~ ~ ~

According to the British Board Of Trade regulations, any ship over 10,000 tons was required to carry sixteen lifeboats, *Titanic* held twenty lifeboats, sixteen being regular wooden boats and four Englehardt collapsible boats, known as A, B, C and D. No ocean liner afloat at that time carried enough lifeboats for all passengers and crew. Prior to the *Titanic* sinking, it was generally believed that the North Atlantic was crowded with vessels. The lifeboats of any stricken vessel would be used to ferry passengers and crew to other rescue vessels that would be summoned by radio to the stricken ship. It was also believed, any large vessel in danger would be able to stay afloat for hours, in some cases, days, before all passengers and crew were rescued.

Titanic's lifeboats were built by Harland and Wolff, and installed in January 1912. These were supported by a new design of davit, which allowed two or three lifeboats to use the same davit. This would have allowed for more lifeboats to be carried. Harland and Wolff had proposed the fitting of 64 lifeboats, but later designs provided for only 32 boats. After consultations with White Star Line, the number had halved again, to a mere 16 boats, plus the four Engelhardt collapsibles.

The almost completed *Titanic* was dry docked in Belfast Harbour, in the Thomson Graving Dock on February 3rd 1912, where she was fitted with her three propellers and a final coat of paint. From her bottom to just above the water line, she was coated with red anti-fouling paint. The rest of her hull was painted black, her superstructure was painted white. The funnels were White Star Line's traditional beige with a band of black on top.

In early March 1912, *Titanic* was removed from the dry dock, to make room for repairs to be made again to *Olympic*, which had lost a propeller to an underwater obstruction. To quicken *Olympic*'s repair, the starboard propeller was removed from *Titanic* and installed on *Olympic*. By the end of March, a new starboard propeller was fitted to *Titanic*. *Titanic*'s construction and fitting out was finally completed.

Titanic's sea trials were due to begin on April 1st 1912. Various members of her crew had begun to arrive at Belfast throughout March, many of them engineers, who had to familiarise themselves with the ships brand new, vast machinery. The junior officers - Pitman, Boxhall, Lowe and Moody - had arrived on March 27th, they had orders to report to Chief Officer William Murdoch, who was already onboard with Second Officer Charles Lightoller.

Sea Trials

Originally scheduled for the 1st April 1912, *Titanic's* sea trial were postponed due to unfavourable weather conditions, as it was believed sailing her down the narrow channel of the River Lagan would be too hazardous. Reluctantly, the trials were delayed until the following day. This meant there would be one day less to stock the ship with provisions and supplies before her maiden voyage on April 10th. Many crew and Officers took the opportunity to familiarise themselves further with the new mammoth ship.

Titanic leaving Belfast Harbour for her Sea Trials on April 2, 1912

Monday, April 2nd 1912, dawned clear enough to undertake the trials. Crowds were gathering on the river banks by 6am, to witness *Titanic's* grand passage under the command of Captain Charles Bartlett. Also aboard were 78 stokers, greasers and firemen, 41 other crew, as well as representatives of various companies. Harland and Wolff were represented by Thomas Andrews and Edward Wilding, while Harold S. Sanderson represented the International Mercantile Marine Company. Jack Philips and Harold Bride were also on board as Marconi wireless operators to 'fine tune' the radio equipment. Lord Pirrie and Bruce Ismay were not present, because of illness. Also present was Francis Caruthers, a surveyor from the Board Of Trade, to see that everything worked and that the ship was fit to carry passengers.

Shortly before 6am, Harland and Wolff's own tug, *Hercules* had the honour of getting the first line aboard *Titanic*. The other tugs took their respective positions, *Huskisson* at the port side of the stern, *Herculaneum* at the starboard at the stern, *Hornby* was stationed on the starboard bowline and *Herald* pulled the forward line.

The grand ship's mooring lines were dropped then, at the sound of the whistle from *Herculaneum*, the accompanying tugs all took up the slack in the ropes. *Titanic* was moved away from the jetty into the middle of the river. She was soon moving forward as the crowds that had gathered on the river banks, started cheering her progress as she moved gracefully down the Belfast Lough, until she was two miles off Carrickfergus. The tugs that provided the power for the last two miles stopped, casting off their tow lines, now stood back as a blue and white burgee was raised, indicating to all the observers present on the banks, on the tugs and all else witnessing this moment in history; "I am undergoing sea trials". The bells rang out from the telegraph, across the bridge and reverberated deep down in the engine room. This was the moment of truth. Excitement rang out as the valves were opened, sending steam from the boilers to the two huge engines. Slowly at the start but surely. *Titanic's* propellers were turning. The great monument to man's achievement was under her own power, for the first time in her short life.

According to the British Board Of Trade regulations, testing was first carried out in Belfast Lough, consisting of a number of tests of her handling characteristics. Then *Titanic* went out to open waters in the Irish Sea, for the next phase of testing that was to last the next twelve hours. These tests consisted of the vessel being driven at differing speeds, testing her turning abilities. Then suddenly stopping the ship with the engines at full astern. Also known as 'Crash Stopping' this test brought her to a complete stop in 850 yards or 777 metres, in 3 minutes and 15 seconds. In total, *Titanic* covered a distance of about 80 nautical miles or 150 kilometres, averaging 18 knots.

Titanic returned to Belfast at about 7pm, the surveyor signed an "Agreement and Account of Voyages and Crew", valid for 12 months. *Titanic* had passed her sea trials. She could now sail to Southampton and prepare for her maiden voyage to New York, as scheduled, on April 10, 1912.

CHAPTER THREE

Southampton

This is a marvelous ship and I feel very disappointed I am not to make the first voyage.

-David Blair, original Second Officer, R.M.S. Titanic.

After the completion of her Sea trials from Belfast on April 2, *Titanic* sailed to Southampton at 8pm, where she was moored at White Star Berth 44, on Wednesday April 3rd, 1912.

Both *Olympic* and *Titanic* were registered in Liverpool as their home port. The offices of both White Star Line and Cunard were situated in Liverpool. Cunard's two star attractions on the North Atlantic route, *Lusitania* and *Mauritania* sailed out of Liverpool, followed by a port of call in Ireland, before embarking on the Trans-Atlantic run to New York. The Olympic-class liners of White Star line were to sail out of Southampton on England's southern coast. White Star realised Southampton had many advantages over Liverpool, mainly Southampton's closer proximity to London and Northern France, to which the Olympic-class liners could easily cross the channel, using Cherbourg to embark clientele from Continental Europe before crossing the channel again to Queenstown, Southern Ireland. The Southampton, Cherbourg-New York run became so popular that after the cessation of WWI, most British ocean liners began using Southampton as their physical home port, while retaining Liverpool as their Port of Registration as a mark of respect until the early 1960s. Cunard Lines Queen Elizabeth 2 was the first British Ocean Liner to be registered at Southampton when introduced into service in 1969.

The Loading of supplies and provisions to *Titanic* began on April 3 for her maiden voyage to New York, beginning on Wednesday 10 April.

By Saturday 6 April, the general cargo of 560 tons was arriving at White Star Berth 44, for loading aboard *Titanic*. White Star Line's hiring hall was packed with the British Seafarers Union and National Sailors and Fireman's Union members, all wishing to get back to work, as the 1912 coal strike had caused widespread unemployment among the Southampton sailors. The majority of *Titanic's* crew came from Southampton, with a few coming from Liverpool, London and Belfast. By the end of the day, the majority of the operating crew had been hired and signed on.

The required 5,800 tons of coal was loaded through the side coaling ports, which for a ship the size of *Titanic* was a massive task, taking 24 hours before the ship's carpenter would seal up the coal ports with a buckram gasket soaked in red lead. This was followed by the painstaking task of cleaning the coal dust off handrailings, decks, staircases and passageways, all of which had to be cleaned thoroughly to remove the fine coating of coal dust that spread everywhere.

Easter Sunday, 7 April, was a quiet day for *Titanic*. The mining strike had ended the day before on the 6th April. There wasn't time to ship newly mined coal to Southampton in time for *Titanic's* maiden voyage. Coal from five Mercantile Marine company vessels had been loaded onto *Titanic*, together with excess coal from her sister ship *Olympic*. *Titanic's* blue ensign fluttered from the stern flagpole throughout Easter Sunday and the ship's bell rung out every passing hour.

Monday 8th April, with only three days to go before her maiden voyage. Activity on Berth 44 was beginning to become frantic as fresh food and supplies were arriving by train and being taken onboard. Seventy five thousand pounds of fresh meat, eleven thousand pounds of fresh fish and 1,750 Quarts of ice cream were put into the large refrigerators on Orlop deck aft. Thomas Andrews was also onboard throughout the day to oversee last minute details and to rectify any slight problems that may have occurred during the trip from

Belfast to Southampton. Andrews remained onboard until 6.30pm.

Tuesday 9th April, Food continued to be loaded onto *Titanic*, her last full day in port before her maiden voyage tomorrow. Captain Clark from the Board of Trade was onboard inspecting just about every part of the ship, to which Second Officer Charles Lightoller remarked: " He did his job, and I'll say he did it thoroughly". The new Captain, Edward J Smith made his own inspection of the ship. While Smith visited the bridge, a London photographer snapped his picture.

That picture became forever immortalised, as it is the only picture taken of Captain Smith on the bridge of his last command. *Titanic's* last night in port is quiet and cold, with only a skeleton crew onboard.

Literary Predictions

Over a century since *Titanic* sank, many stories and books have come to the surface claiming to have predicted the great liners demise. Books written before and during her construction and fitting out at Belfast are believed to describe accurately, what was in store for those who perished, including one of the authors himself, whose book is believed to have predicted his own death, when he joined the many who would witness *Titanic's* maiden voyage from Southampton to New York during the bleak month of April 1912.

Arthur Paintin

One prediction is believed to be from a Steward, just days before the ships date with destiny, being from Steward Arthur Paintin - Captain Smith's personal steward - who after *Titanic*'s departure from Southampton and close shave with the moored liner *New York*, wrote a letter home to his family. When *Titanic* arrived at Queenstown, Paintin mailed his letter home. The letter stated:

"My Dear Mother and Father,"

"Many thanks for your nice long letter this morning, received before leaving. I intended writing before we left, but there did not seem time for everything. I cannot realise that I had ten days at home, and am very sorry I could not get to Oxford for we have now commenced the quick voyages all the summer (bar accidents). I say that because the Olympic's bad luck seems to have followed us for as we came out of Southampton dock this morning we passed quite close to the New York which was tied up in the Adriatic's old berth, and whether it was suction or what it was I don't know, but the New York's ropes snapped like a piece of cotton and she drifted against us. There was great excitement for some little time, but I don't think there was any damage done bar one or two people knocked over by the ropes."

"Bai jove what a fine ship this is, much better than the Olympic as far as passengers are concerned. But my little room is nothing near so nice, no daylight, electric light on all day, but I suppose it's no use grumbling."

Paintin's job was to be at the beck and call of Smith. He had transferred with Smith to *Titanic* from *Olympic* for The maiden voyage and so would have known Smith better than most people onboard *Titanic*. Arthur Paintin was last seen, according to some testimonies, standing beside Captain Smith on the bridge just before the vessel's long plunge into the North-Atlantic Ocean.

Letter from Steward, Arthur Paintin to his family, addressed from RMS Titanic.

W. T. Stead

Another passenger, English Journalist W.T. Stead, got mentioned with another prediction several years before his fictional book mentions his own demise. In 1886, Stead's story '*How The Mail Steamer Went Down In Mid Atlantic - By A Survivor*', mentions an ocean liner, which leaves Liverpool and becomes involved in a collision with an iceberg on its journey to New York. In the ensuing panic, the ship's Captain brandishes a revolver to prevent steerage passengers from storming the boat deck. Many passengers are lost, due to too few lifeboats. The story portrays its hero as calmly going down with the ship while smoking in the smoking room.

It appears that his fictional work did not dissuade him from embarking on trans-Atlantic voyages himself. W. T. Stead was a pioneer in Investigative journalism and was a controversial figure during the Victorian era. He is also featured in the myth of *Titanic's* mummy.

W.T. Stead

This myth also includes a story of Stead going down onboard *Titanic*, quietly and fearlessly reading in the smoking room. The 1958 movie '*A Night To Remember*', also includes a part where Stead is portrayed as reading a book in the smoking room as the great ship slides below the surface. A fellow survivor, Philip Mock contradicts this story by claiming he saw Stead clinging to a raft with John Jacob Astor. Mock stated that both Astor and Stead had their feet dangling in the water until "their feet became frozen, and they were compelled to release their hold. Both were drowned."

However, it is the story of Stead as a hero as portrayed in Walter Lord's, *'A Night To Remember'* that persists to this day.

The Wreck Of The Titan, or Futility.

After retiring from a life at sea in 1894, Morgan Robertson began writing short stories. One story he began writing in 1897 would become famous for its prediction of the loss of the greatest ocean liner in the world.

His novel, *The Wreck Of The Titan, Or Futility* would propel him into stardom as an author who had predicted the *Titanic* disaster.

With the assistance of what he would refer to as his "astral writing partner", Robertson set about writing his story that included a triple screwed 75.000 ton vessel, the like of which the world had never seen before, ploughing through the fog and icy North Atlantic ocean on her maiden voyage, at speeds of 25 knots on a moonless April night, before colliding with an iceberg. The name of the vessel was "*Titan*".

Robertson's *Titan* was 800 feet in length and her 19 water-tight compartments provided her passengers with the illusion of safety, giving his mythical ship the popular belief she was "unsinkable". The majority of *Titan's* passengers and crew would drown, because there were only twenty-four lifeboats.

This is, however, as far as fiction and reality coincide. Robertson was an experienced seaman, giving him plenty of scope for writing based on accurate maritime knowledge and trends because he would have been very well aware of modern ship-building at that time. Including the technological features, such behemoth vessels required for modern safety at sea. Giving Robertson plenty of material to write about imagined disasters at sea.

'The Wreck Of The Titan' does not concentrate on the vessel, but is more the story of a naval Officer who finds God and manages to fight his alcoholism, while managing to win back the love of his life. While also managing to slay a polar bear in order to save a small child.

After *Titanic* sank, Robertson was acclaimed for his clairvoyance which he denied, later stating: "No, I know what I am writing about, thats all".

Many other books were published, claiming to have predicted *Titanic's* demise with accuracy. Among them were the 1908 book called *'The Ship's Run'*, by Bodkin M. O'Donnell, which featured the largest, most luxurious ship afloat. Bodkin even named his ship "*Titanic*," which sank. The construction of the actual *Titanic* was underway by 1908 and it is almost certain that *Titanic* featured in the research for his material.

Another short story under the pen name of Mayn Clew Garnett, *'The White Ghost Of Disaster'*, was published in 1912, by Thornton Jenkins Hains. The story featured an 800 foot ocean liner called *'Admiral'*. While traveling through the North Atlantic Ocean at a speed of 22.5 knots, *'Admiral'* suddenly hits an iceberg and sinks. Again, the majority of passengers and crew are lost due to a shortage of lifeboats.

At the same time *Titanic* sank, *'The White Ghost Of Disaster'* was appearing on newsstands in the pages of *Popular Magazine*.

~ ~ ~ ~

Wednesday 10th April, The weather overnight at Southampton was dry and the morning dawned fine. The forecast stated that the day was going to be dry and sunny with patchy cloud. The early morning temperature was a cool 4.4° C. The maximum temperature would reach 11.7° C with a chilly northwesterly wind.

Captain Smith, *Titanic's* new master, had boarded at 7am. Captain E. J. Smith was a man of the sea for over forty years. He had previously commanded some of White Star Lines finest ships, including *RMS Olympic* on her maiden voyage. He was known as the millionaires Captain, because he was extremely popular with White Star Line's wealthier passengers. He was well liked by the crew who worked under him.

As White Star Lines Commodore Of The Line, Smith's salary of $6,250 was twice that of other Captains, making him 'The Captain Of All Captains'. Although Smith had decided it was time for him to retire, he had stayed on at the request of Bruce Ismay. Smith had decided to wait until White Star Line had a bigger, more refined ship. Some sources say that ship may have been the upcoming launch and maiden voyage of

R.M.S. Britannic, as opposed to the popular belief that he was going to retire after the maiden voyage of *Titanic.*

The docks of Southampton were buzzing with activity on the morning of April 10th 1912. Crates of supplies were still being lifted into the holds. People were arriving from all over England, to see her before the ship departed later at noon. Motor cars were arriving and dropping off passengers who were preparing to board the enormous ship berthed at White Star Line berth 44.

At 8am the Officers were assembled on deck, where an informal lifeboat drill was held in the presence of Captain Clarke of the British Board Of Trade. Fourth Officer Joseph Boxhall testified: "The crew were mustered and when the names were called the boats were lowered in the presence of the Board of Trade surveyors." Two of her lifeboats, lifeboats 11 and 15 from the starboard side were loaded with crew members and swung out, according to fifth Officer Harold Lowe, both were lowered to the water. "We were lowered down in the boats with a boat's crew. The boats were manned, and we rowed around a couple of turns, and then came back and were hoisted up and had breakfast, and then went about our duties." the lifeboat drill was performed to satisfy the Board Of Trades regulations, certifying *Titanic* was a migrant ship. According to Lowe, the whole process took about 20 minutes to half an hour.

Second Officer Charles Lightoller later testified at the British Wreck Commissioners Inquiry, when questioned by Mr. Clement Edwards - Question number 14657 to 14662 - regarding the Lifeboat drill on 10 April 1912:

14657. On the day you sailed did you make a test of the boats and the apparatus?
Lightoller - Yes.

14658. In the presence of Captain Clark?
Lightoller - Yes.

14659. It was intended as a formal inspection by the Board of Trade?
Lightoller - Yes.

14660. Now, do you remember the extent to which you carried out the test?
Lightoller - Yes, with regard to the boats.

14661. What did you do?
Lightoller - We lowered two boats, that is swung out, carried on with the crew, swung out the boats, lowering away, placing the crew in the boats, the crews with their lifebelts on, lowered the boats, released them, sent them out, brought them back to the ship, and hoisted them inboard again and secured them.

14662. How many (Lifeboats)?
Lightoller - Two.

Due to the informality of the lifeboat drill, it's very unlikely the majority of the crew witnessed this drill, as it was the only lifeboat drill of its type conducted on

Titanic. The crew members then tended to their duties before the passengers started to board.

At about the same time as the crew were boarding *Titanic*, the London and South Western boat train was leaving London's Waterloo station to travel the 80 miles to Southampton with some of the Second and Third class passengers who were to board *Titanic* for a new life in The Promised Land. Upon its arrival at the Southampton Terminus, right beside *Titanic* at 9.30am, those passengers were transferred straight onto the ship.

Top from left - 2nd Class passengers boarding, Third Class passengers boarding *Titanic*.
Bottom from left - Third Class Common Room, Passengers boarding at Queenstown.

885 crew members were assigned to *Titanic* for her maiden voyage to New York city. Like many ships of her time, *Titanic* did not have any permanent crew. The majority of the 'casual' crew had come aboard only a

few hours before her departure time and had to be 'signed on'. The process of 'signing on' had begun on the 23rd March, with some crew members being sent to Belfast, working as part of the skeleton crew during her Sea trials and her passage to Southampton.

Captain Edward John Smith was the most senior of the White Star line Captains. He was transferred to *Titanic* from her older sister, *RMS Olympic*. First Officer William McMaster Murdoch was the most senior officer of that rank. First Officer Charles Lightoller was demoted to Second Officer.

A lone figure strolls the promenade deck of Titanic. Believed to be Captain Smith

The crew of *Titanic* were divided into three principle departments: Deck, which consisted of 66 crew; Engine, with 325 and Victualling, with 494 crew members, making the remaining majority of crew, not seamen, although they consisted of Firemen or Stokers,

Engineers, responsible for looking after the engines, or stewards and galley staff, responsible for the passengers, the galley staff being 97% male and 3% being female, who were mainly stewardesses. The other crew members represented a great variety of professions: bakers, butchers, chefs, fishmongers, dishwashers, stewards, laundrymen. cleaners, bedmakers, gymnasium instructors, waiters and a printer, who produced the daily onboard newspaper from items of news, received by the ships wireless operators. *Titanic's* onboard newspaper was called '*Atlantic Daily Bulletin.*'

The majority of the crew were signed on in Southampton on 6 April, with 699 crew members, or 40%, being native to Southampton. A few specialist crew member were either self employed or sub-contractors. This included the five postal clerks for the Royal Mail and United States Post Office Department, the staff of the First Class A La Carte Restaurant and the Café Parisienne, the radio operators, who were employees of Marconi, and the eight self-employed musicians, who travelled in Second Class.

Crew pay varied considerably. Captain Smith was receiving £105 per month, which is equivalent to £7,704 today. stewardesses earned £3,10s, which is £257 today.

Victualling were the lowest paid, though the lowest paid could suppliment their pay substantially through tips from passengers.

At 10am, the first passengers began boarding the ship. Third class passengers were subjected to medical inspection before being allowed onboard. Checking for lice and infectous diseases. Also for ailments and physical impairments that might lead to them being refused entry into the United States. Carrying passengers across the Atlantic, only for them to be refused entry into the US was not a prospect White Star wished for, as they would have to carry them back across the Atlantic. They were then given directions to Third Class cabins and facilities, then shuffled onboard by gangplanks to the lower decks. Single Third Class passengers were separated, the women stayed toward the stern of the ship and men were berthed in the lower decks in the bow of the ship. Families were allowed to board together. Second Class passengers boarded through raised gangways, as did the First Class passengers. 922 passengers were recorded as having boarded *Titanic* at Southampton. The rest boarded the ship at Cherbourg and Queenstown.

A national coal strike in the United Kingdom during the spring of 1912 had already disrupted many schedules to the United States, causing many sailings to be cancelled.

Although the coal strike ended only a few days before *Titanic's* scheduled departure, Her coal had been transferred from other ships, berthed at Southampton, contributing ships being, among others, the *New York, Oceanic* and her sister, *Olympic*. Typically, the maiden voyage for such a prestigous vessel as *Titanic* would carry its full capacity of passengers. *Titanic* could accommodate up to 2,566 passengers. 1,034 from First Class, 510 from Second Class and 1,022 from Third

Class. For her maiden voyage, *Titanic* was carrying 1,317 passengers, consisting of: 324 from First Class, 284 from Second Class and 709 from Third Class. 869 were male, 447 were female. Including 107 children, the largest number being from Third Class.

The exact number of passengers onboard *Titanic* can never be accurately recorded as not all passengers who departed Southampton stayed on for the entire journey. Some disembarked at Cherbourg and Queenstown. Some others had cancelled their bookings because of the coal strike and some didn't turn up for the scheduled departure. 50 booked passengers had cancelled for various reasons. Fares varied, depending on class. Third Class fares from London, Southampton or Queenstown cost £7 5s, equivalent to £532 today, while the cheapest First Class fare cost £23, or £1,677 today. The most expensive First Class suite cost up to £870 or £63,837 today.

Some influencial and prominent people were on *Titanic* as she departed Southampton, because the maiden voyage of such a prestigous vessel was seen as an important social event on the calender. Among them were American Industrialist Benjamin Guggenheim, Businessman and cricketer John Borland Thayer with his wife, Marion with their son Jack, the Countess of Rothes, author and socialite Helen Churchill Candee, journalist William Thomas Stead and Jacques Futrelle and wife May. A silent movie actress, Dorothy Gibson, Montreal Investment Banker Hudson J. C. Allison, his wife Bess and their two children Loraine and Trevor, London Science teacher Lawrence Beasly, New York housewife Mary Jerwan, Arthur Ryerson and his wife

Emily. Also onboard were White Star Lines managing director J, Bruce Ismay and Harland & Wolff's chief designer Thomas Andrews and nine others who were known as Harland and Wolff Guarantee group, comprising of: 3 draughtsmen of which Andrews was the Chief, 4 Fitters, 1 Plumber, 1 Electrician and 1 Apprentice Electrician, who were onboard to assess the general performance of the vessel and observe any problems that could be rectified before the third of the Olympic-class vessels, *Britannic* was finished and ready for service.

Among the passengers who cancelled at the last minute was J. P Morgan from the International Mercantile Marine company. American novelist, Theodore Dreiser - because his Publisher persuaded him to take another ship as it would be cheaper, the Italian inventor of the Marconi wireless system, Guglielmo Marconi - who apparently had paper work to do after taking *Lusitania* three days earlier, Milton Hershey - the man behind the famous Hershey chocolate bar. while returning from a holiday in France and after paying a 10% deposit for the passage on *Titanic*, cancelled and boarded the German Liner, *Amerika*, Pittsburgh steel baron, Henry Frick - who decided to stay in Italy after his wife sprained her ankle and was hospitalised, the 34 year old heir to the Vanderbilt shipping and railroad empire, Alfred Gwynne Vanderbilt, Vanderbilt lived long enough to become a victim of the *Lusitania* sinking, three years later and influential evangelist John R. Mott, who instead took the liner *Lapland*.

Steerage passengers blocked access to lifeboats

Steerage accommodation on *Titanic* was superb, as compared to conditions third class passengers were used to. *Titanic* offered features that were unparalleled on Trans-Atlantic vessels before her, facilities and conditions the Third Class passengers had never seen or experienced before. Steerage cabins were small, but offered luxuries, such as electric lighting and comfortable bunks, personal washing facilities, nightstands and stowage facilities for luggage, and large mess halls for both dining and relaxation.

The pecking order on Trans-Atlantic vessels reflected the Victorian Class system. Every aspect of a passenger's experience reflected that fact. First Class occupied the upper decks, which coincidentally were also where the lifeboats were stationed. Second Class occupied the decks below First Class. Third Class occupied the lower decks.

Stories, books and movies on *Titanic* claim the Third-Class passengers were blocked below decks, in an attempt by the officers to ensure upper class passengers were granted unhindered priority to the lifeboats. It is true that gates were used to prevent steerage passengers from mixing with other classes on *Titanic*, but this was not in anticipation of any emergency. The gates were provided by regulation set out by the American immigration laws to prevent any feared spread of infectious diseases.

Under American Immigration legislation, immigrants had to be kept separate, before processing and health checks. *Titanic* would have first stopped at Ellis Island, where the immigrants would have disembarked for health and immigration processing, before the ship proceeded to its berthing facilities in Manhattan.

Gates separating third class from the rest of the ship were always locked at night on Trans-Atlantic steamers. The night of April 14 1912, being no exception. The claim of Third Class passengers being forcibly detained below decks, has no historical evidence of support.

Steerage passengers on *Titanic* consisted of those from the British Isles, Armenians, Syrians, Chinese, Dutch, Italians, Scandinavians and Russians, the majority speaking in their own languages. Steerage Stewards on *Titanic* were all English speaking. Most historians forget that this in itself presented massive communication problems at any time, but particularly in the panic conditions that existed on the night of April 14.

Most passengers from all classes and the crew believed *Titanic* was "as solid as a rock." Captain Smith never issued an abandon ship order. The first lifeboat wasn't launched until an hour after the ship struck the iceberg. The majority of the passengers and crew were unaware, *Titanic* was in imminent danger. There had been no lifeboat drill since she had left Southampton, ensuring that no passengers knew where their assigned lifeboats were situated. Smith also made no attempt to ensure the boats did not leave half full and no crew members were sure enough to know exactly where they were supposed to be in the event of an emergency or what they were required to do.

Passengers on the lower decks were immediately faced with a labyrinth of passages and corridors to reach the boat deck. First and Second class were most likely to reach the lifeboats with ease, as they were launched from the First and Second class promenade decks. Confusion reigned on *Titanic* immediately after she struck the berg. Sadly, before it was realised by the Stewards that some gates were still locked, half the number of lifeboats had already left the ship.

No Third-Class passengers gave testimony at the following inquiries into the *Titanic* disaster. A report from the British Board Of Trade inquiry stated, claims that Third-Class passengers were blocked access to the boat decks were false. The BOT report also noted that *Titanic* was in compliance with the American Immigration laws although the evidence noted that initially, some of the gates remained locked in compliance with the American Immigration laws, while stewards waited for instructions to open them.

The Chair of the Inquiry, Lord Mersey, noted that many third class passengers were reluctant to leave the ship, "unwilling to part with their baggage", and had difficulty getting from their quarters to the lifeboats.

Representing Third-Class at the British Inquiry was W D Harbinson. Harbinson concluded "No evidence has been given in the course of this case that would substantiate a charge that any attempt was made to keep back the third class passengers."

Yet the myth persists.

~ ~ ~ ~

Top left to right - Benjamin Guggenheim, John Jacob Astor IV and Margaret Astor, Isidor and Ida Strauss.
Bottom left to right - Margaret Brown, Dorothy Gibson, John Thayer

Over the years since the disaster, many people have claimed to have "just missed the boat." On April 20 1912, Michigan's *Sault Sainte Marie Evening News* newspaper headlined all 6,904 of them that have been included in what has come to be known as "The just missed it club", consisting of 3,478 Americans, 2,050 Britons and a scattering of 476 from other countries. It appears that 4,965 of those had previously paid their passage on *Titanic,* but cancelled before the great ship sailed, 892 apparently had premonitions about a disaster and the rest were apparently in Paris at the trime and couldn't get away.

Titanic's capacity was 3,547 passengers and crew. *Titanic* entered the North Atlantic carrying 2,208 passengers and crew. It's doubtful that she would have been able to accommodate another 6,904 passengers onboard without sinking! But over the years since, I suppose many fireside chats have been told of how Grandfather's ancestor "Just missed it". On April 26 2012, according to Ohio's Lima Daily News, the number had dramatically increased to 118,337, who were all proud members of the "Just Missed It Club".

Titanic departing White Star Line Berth 44. 12pm, April 10, 1912

Just before midday, the Blue Peter Pennant was hoisted on *Titanic's* foremast, announcing the ships imminent departure. The triple-valve whistle was sounded three times, the gangplanks and gangways were withdrawn, the tugs that would tow the massive vessel out into mid stream of the Southampton dock were already in place. The lines that held *Titanic* to the dock were cast off, the tugs tugged and heaved at the ship, coordinating their work with a series of whistles, until they reached deeper water and the tow lines were dropped from *Titanic*. The crowds that had gathered to farewell her passengers began to cheer to the passengers who had massed on the Port side decks. The ships telegraph rang out, the massive liners propellers began turning. *Titanic's* maiden voyage had begun.

As *Titanic* made her way gracefully down the River Test, on which Southampton dock is built, the propellers churning up the water were creating problems. Two other vessels were berthed beside each other at their pier. *Oceanic* was closest to the pier and the *New York* was closest to *Titanic's* path. As the massive wash from *Titanic* struck them, the *New York* rose high in the water, then dropped back down with enough force to snap her mooring ropes. Many of the spectators and relatives shouting and waving their goodbyes to those onboard *Titanic*, were forced to run clear as the thick mooring ropes snaked up and down, then whiplashed back onto the dock. The stern of the *New York* began to swing out towards the huge *Titanic*, while crew members on *New York* ran up and down the length of the hull, securing ropes, blankets and mats to protect the vessel from the possible collision. The Captain of the tug, *Vulcan*, who had moments earlier disconnected from *Titanic*, managed to get a line onto the *New York* as she began slowly creeping towards *Titanic*.

Noticing the perilous situation his ship was in, Captain Smith ordered the ship, Full Astern, to try and lessen the pulling effect *Titanic* was having on the *New York*. This action created another wash that pushed the *New York* out of contact with *Titanic*. Both ships came within four feet or 1.2 m of each other. The excitement was not yet over. As *New York* turned, her Bow now facing the dock, she slowly began moving towards *Teutonic*, moored to the side. *New York* struck *Teutonic* slightly, without damage. The tug *Vulcan,* and another tug managed to manouvre *New York* back into her mooring as *Titanic* continued to limp past and clear.

The incident was familiar to Captain Smith, as only seven months earlier, the ship he was commanding, *Titanic's* older sister *Olympic,* was involved in a similar incident with the Royal Navy cruiser *HMS Hawke*. *RMS Olympic* and *Hawke* were travelling on a parallel course, when all of a sudden, *HMS Hawke* found herself being dragged into *Olympic's* side. After the conseguent collision, *RMS Olympic's* hull was pierced below and above the waterline, breaching two of her watertight compartments. *HMS Hawke's* bow was crushed. Although no one was seriously injured, the blame was placed on Captain Smith. Serious questions were being asked about the handling of these massive vessels in shallow coastal waters. Repairs to *Olympic* delayed *Titanic's* completion at Harland and Wolff.

Titanic and the New York. Danger narrowly averted

The main topic of conversation at that point from the passengers on *Titanic*, who were witnessing the events as they unfolded was, just how a massive ship could create a suction that could attract another vessel in the same manner as the *Olympic/Hawke* collision. This event, seemed to have confirmed a theory that had been advanced in news articles from the law courts. The 'suction theory', first advanced by the British Admiralty, was scoffed at by the public, but this event seems to have confirmed the British Admiralty's theory.

With the narrow escape from danger behind her, *Titanic* entered the English Channel, moving past the Isle of Wight on her starboard side, onward to her first port of call on her voyage to New York City: Cherbourg, Northern France.

CHAPTER FOUR

Cherbourg To Queenstown

This ship is a monstrous floating Babylon

- Journalist, William Stead

*T*itanic arrived in Cherbourg, Northern France at 6pm, April 10 1912, at about the same time, the French Liner *SS Niagara* struck an iceberg, south of New Foundland, while traveling to New York in thick fog. At the time of the collision, the ship had been traveling at a reduced speed as she had been in an ice field since the afternoon. The *Niagara* Captain Juham, sent out an S.O.S. wireless message immediately after the collision, asking for immediate assistance. Upon inspection of his ship, he found: although water was leaking in due to buckling of the plates below the waterline, it was in no immediate danger. So he sent out another wireless message saying he could make his own way to New York.

Upon *Niagara's* arrival in New York, there was little evidence she was badly damaged except for some water in her hold.

As the sun was sinking on the horizon, giving the chalk cliffs of the French coast a reddish glow, a lighthouse perched on the end of a large breakwater indicated *Titanic's* entrance into Cherbourg Harbour.

Captain Smith and the Senior Officers of Titanic.

Back row: Chief Purser Herbert McElroy, 2nd Officer Charles Lightoller, 3rd Officer Herbert Pitman, 4th Officer Joseph Boxhall, 5th Officer Harold Lowe.

Front row: 6th Officer James Moody, Chief Officer Henry Wilde, Captain Edward Smith, 1st Officer William Murdoch.

Originally scheduled to arrive at Cherbourg, the largest artificial harbour in the world at 5.00pm on 10 April 1912, *Titanic* was running over an hour late, because of her near miss with the *New York* while leaving Southampton. After her five-hour journey to Northern France, she finally arrived at 6.30pm. Cherbourg is not a deep-water port, so was not able to accommodate the large steamers. *Titanic* had to drop anchor in the Roads, just off the Cap de la Hogue, near the Central fort in Cherbourg, while White Star Line's Tenders *Nomadic* and *Traffic*, both built at Harland and Wolff to cater for the large liners at Cherbourg, ferried more passengers, luggage and mail out to *Titanic*.

A late afternoon squall had built up near Cherbourg Harbour, making the two tenders bounce rather alarmingly towards the massive hull and striking the side of the ship occasionally. Never-the-less, the new passengers, luggage and mail were taken onboard without incident.

Among the 281 new passengers to board at Cherbourg were, the twice married, American billionaire, John Jacob Astor IV with his new wife, Madeleine Talmage Astor and Mrs Astor's nurse. Millionairess Margaret Brown, who is now better known as 'the unsinkable Molly Brown' and the Scottish baron and financial director, Sir Cosmo Edmund Duff-Gordon and his wife Lady Lucy Christiana Duff-Gordon also boarded at Cherbourg. At 9.00pm *Titanic* was ready for the next leg of her journey, the overnight sailing to Queenstown, Southern Ireland.

As *Titanic* departed, leaving Cherbourg behind her, the more experienced trans-Atlantic travelers settled into familiar routines. While the new travelers wandered the ship, taking in the marvelous splendours of the new ship. As the First class passengers were sipping their after-dinner liqueurs and coffee, the ships orchestra began playing an impromptu concert on A Deck, the first of what was to become a nightly occurrence. By 11.00pm, the concert had run its course. Some of the passengers continued to explore the vessel, and to relax with friends in one of the smoking rooms and lounges, while others decided to retire for the night.

A child - 6 yr. old, Robert Douglas Spedden, playing with a spinning-top onboard Titanic. Robert survived the Titanic sinking but was tragically killed in a road traffic accident in New York on 8th August 1915.

Titanic's Mummy

According to this myth, the mummy of an ancient Egyptian Priestess of the Pharaoh Amen-Ra, was placed near the ships bridge in her sarcophagus instead of in the cargo hold. The influence of this ancient priestess affected Captain Smith's reasoning, subsequently causing him to ignore numerous ice warnings and to fail to order the ship to slow down, before and after the collision with the iceberg thus dooming *Titanic* to a disastrous end.

During *Titanic's* maiden voyage, famous journalist and spiritualist, William T, Stead, told the story of Amen-Ra to a group of passengers who had met to discuss the meaning of life. The story, as told by Stead, was as follows:

After the discovery of the Mummy in the early 1890s in Egypt, the purchaser of the Mummy ran into serious misfortune. The Mummy was subsequently donated to the British Museum where it continued to be the cause of mysteries and problems for both the museum's visitors and staff. Eventually, the Mummy was purchased by William Thomas Stead, who dismissed the claims of a curse as, quirks of circumstance. According to Stead, he arranged for the mummy to be concealed under his car, fearing that, because of its reputation, it would not otherwise be taken onboard the *Titanic*.

The meeting spawned curiosity among the attending passengers, who wondered if the Mummy was actually on the vessel. After the disaster, many imagined, fabricated stories were born and published in the press as *Titanic's* 'Mummy Passenger'. The Mummy of the Priestess of Amen-Ra was actually still on display at the British Museum in London - who had owned it since 1889 - at the time of the *Titanic* sinking.

The only survivor of the group of eight who were told the original story by William T. Stead, was Frederick K. Steward, who had sat next to Stead at *Titanic's* saloon table, was later asked about the Mummy story and replied that he would not dare repeat the story told by Stead. After transferring to *Carpathia* following *Titanic's* sinking. Steward recounted his meeting with Stead. He said Stead's reason for traveling to America was to assist with the New York campaign of 'The Men And Religion Forward Movement'.

Steward remarked that Stead talked much about spiritualism. He continued, "He told a story of a Mummy case in the British Museum which, he said, had had amazing adventures, but which punished with great calamities any person who wrote its story. He told of one person after another who, he said, had come to grief after writing the story, and added that, although he knew it, he would never write it. He did not say whether ill-luck attached to the mere telling of it."

Since the ship's sinking in 1912, an elaborate story has persevered:

"The Princess of Amen-Ra lived some 1,500 years before Christ. When she died, she was laid in an ornate wooden coffin and buried deep in a vault at Luxor, on the banks of the Nile. In the late 1890s, four rich, young, Englishmen visiting the excavations at Luxor were invited to buy an exquisitely fashioned Mummy case containing the remains of Priestess of Amen-Ra."

"They drew lots. The man who won paid several thousand pounds and had the coffin taken to his hotel. A few hours later, he was seen walking out towards the desert. He never returned. The next day, one of the remaining three men was shot by an Egyptian servant accidentally. His arm was so severely wounded it had to be amputated. The third man in the foursome found on his return home that the bank holding his entire savings had failed. The fourth man suffered a severe illness, lost his job and was reduced to selling matches in the street."

"Nevertheless, the coffin reached England (causing other misfortunes along the way), where it was bought by a London businessman. After three of his family members had been injured in a road accident and his house damaged by fire, the businessman donated the coffin to the British Museum. As the coffin was being unloaded from a truck in the museum courtyard, the truck suddenly went into reverse and trapped a passerby . Then as the casket was being lifted up the stairs by two workmen, one fell and broke his leg. The other, apparently in perfect health, died unaccountably two days later. Once the Priestess was installed in the Egyptian Room, trouble really started. The Museum's night watchmen frequently heard frantic hammering and sobbing from the coffin. Other exhibits in the room were also often hurled about at night. One watchman died on duty; causing the other watchmen wanting to quit and cleaners also refused to go near the Priestess. When a visitor derisively flicked a dust cloth at the face painted on the coffin, his child died of measles soon afterwards.

Finally, the authorities had the Mummy carried down to the basement, figuring it could not do any harm down there. Within a week, one of the helpers was seriously ill, and the supervisor of the move was found dead at his desk."

"By now, the papers had heard of it. A journalist photographer took a picture of the Mummy case and when he developed it, the painting on the coffin was of a horrifying human face. The photographer went home, locked his bedroom door and shot himself".

"Soon afterwards, the Museum sold the Mummy to a private collector. After continual misfortune (and deaths), the owner banished it to the attic. A well known authority on the occult, Madame Helena Blavatsky, visited the premises. Upon entry, she was seized with a shivering fit and searched the house for the source of "an evil influence of incredible intensity". She finally came to the attic and found the Mummy case. "Can you exorcise this evil spirit?" asked the owner. "There is no such thing as exorcism. Evil remains evil forever. Nothing can be done about it. I implore you to get rid of this evil as soon as possible". But no British museum would take the Mummy; the fact that almost 20 people had met with misfortune, disaster or death from handling the casket, in barely 10 yrs., was now well known."

"Eventually, a hard-headed American archaeologist - who dismissed the happenings as quirks of circumstance - paid a handsome price for the Mummy and arranged for its removal to New York. In April of 1912, the new owner escorted its treasure aboard a sparkling, new White Star liner about to make its maiden voyage to New York."

"On the night of April 14, amid scenes of unprecedented horror, the Priestess of Amen-Ra accompanied 1,500 passengers to their deaths at the bottom of the Atlantic. The name of the ship was Titanic..."

What happened next, is not known.

As with many myths, the people mentioned in a good story are not anything other than people. No names are actually mentioned, as names can be verified and confirmed, so when names are not mentioned, verification can never be confirmed, thus making the story just that, a story. One name is mentioned however, the name of Madame Helena Blavatsky. Helena Blavatsky was a scholar of ancient wisdom literature, who was born in the Ukraine, Russia in 1831 and died in the Ukraine in 1891. The previous story placed the Mummy of the Priestess of Amen-Ra as being discovered at Luxor in the 1890s. This makes the chances of a Helena Blavatsky, a Russian citizen, encountering the Mummy in England as being next to impossible.

The Priestess of Amen-Ra, although renowned as 'The Unlucky Mummy', is not actually a Mummy at all. It is, in fact, a painted plaster and wood lid or the inner top of a coffin contained within the sarcophagus. This painted lid of an unidentified woman is 162 centimetres or 64 inches long. The painted surface includes a woman's hands protruding from the plaster covered wooden mummy-board. The original owner is unknown, although the British Museum in London acquired it from someone in 1889. The Mummy board is dated between 950 - 900 B.C. the only times in its history, at the British Museum, it was ever removed from display was during WWI and WWII, when it was put into storage for safety. In 1990, it was temporarily displayed at two venues in Australia and also formed part of an exhibition in Taiwan, at the Taiwan National Palace Museum between 4 February and 27 March 2007, and was also the subject of a press conference, at the same time. The Mummy board is generally displayed in room 62 at the British Museum in London, with the identification number of 22542.

The cover of a Pearson's magazine from 1909, featuring a story of the Mummy.

The British Journalist and Spiritualist William T. Stead did not survive the *Titanic* sinking. He is involved in another *Titanic* Myth, where he had earlier predicted his own death.

~ ~ ~ ~

In the mid morning of 11 April 1912, the grey mountains of Cork, Southern Ireland came within view of *Titanic*, the day was partly cloudy and relatively warm.

   A brisk wind greeted *Titanic* as she graciously slipped into the Harbour at Queenstown at 11.30am, to pick up a further 113 Third Class and seven Second Class passengers, while seven passengers disembarked, including Father Francis Browne, a Jesuit trainee, who had taken many photographs onboard *Titanic*, since her departure from Southampton the previous day. The last known photograph of *Titanic* - that of her departing Cork Harbour is credited to Francis Browne.

Cork Harbour is one of several that lay claim to being the second largest natural harbour in the world, but is unable to cater for large vessels. The two tenders from the White Star office situated at Queenstown, *Ireland* and *America*, would have to ferry the boarding passengers and transport the disembarking passengers to shore. The boarding passengers had started gathering at the White Star Line Office hours before *Titanic*'s arrival. Some trekking as much as twenty miles to reach the ship that was to take them to the New World.

At 1.30pm *Titanic's* whistles let out a long blast shortly before weighing anchor and beginning her westward journey across the Atlantic Ocean.

Queenstown was a seafaring port, with the gathering crowd every bit as knowledgeable and eager as the crowd that had seen *Titanic* off at Southampton. They had watched in admiration as the great ship slid past the heads, then slowly rounded Roche Point, before dropping anchor two miles offshore.

One more, short stop was made at the Daunt Light-ship to drop off the pilot, who had guided the great ship in and out of Cork Harbour. Captain Smith began charting his course into the Atlantic, taking full advantage of the Irish Coast and giving his passengers the full benefit of the glorious view. By mid-afternoon, *Titanic* had cleared the Stags and Kedge Island. By Tea time the Fastnet Light, about 55 nautical miles or 102 kilometres from Queenstown, was in site.

The last known photograph of Titanic as she left Queenstown April 11, 1912.

By nightfall, Ireland was behind them, many of the Irish migrants had gathered on the Poop deck and stern to catch the last glimpses of their homeland.

Many passengers were glimpsing the last sight of land before they were to set foot on American soil, not knowing the experiences that awaited them. Before the

American coastline would be in sight, many experiences to be faced - experiences and memories that would last a lifetime for those lucky enough to see land again. Many good people and loved ones that would have to be mourned.

CHAPTER FIVE

To The New World

> When arranging a tour around the United States I had decided to cross on the *Titanic*. It was rather a novelty to be on the largest ship yet launched. It was no exaggeration to say that it was quite easy to lose one's way on such a ship.
>
> - Lawrence Beesley, Titanic survivor

From the time *Titanic* departed Southampton on 10 April, The passengers and crew were experiencing remarkably sensible weather. From April 10th to the night of April 14, she was experiencing relatively mild temperatures of around 50° F to 60° F or 10° to 15° C, light to moderate winds and mostly rain free skies.

A second, much more potent cold front, with brisk North-West winds of 20 knots lurked to the west. *Titanic* would reach that on the morning of April 14. Obviously, for the season, the air mass was quite cold.

Top left - First Class Lounge. Top right - Third Class Cabin.

Bottom left - B Deck. Bottom. Right - Boat Deck.

As dawn broke on Friday 12 April. *Titanic* was well out into the Atlantic Ocean. Since departing the Irish coast - the evening before, The vessel had covered 386 miles at a steady 21 knots, encouraged by the fine, calm clear weather that was expected to continue over the next few days. Most of the passengers were becoming increasingly admiring towards the new ship. The way she was behaving, the total absence of vibrations, the smooth travel and her overall stability. White Star Line seems to have spared no expense toward the comfort of its passengers. For which Second Officer Lightoller would comment: " we are not out to make a record passage; in fact the White Star Line invariably run their ships at reduced speed for the first few voyages."

Passenger, Science teacher Lawrence Beesley commented that the wind was very cold, generally too cold to sit out on deck to read or write, so many spent a good deal of time in the library. Beesley also commented on the way the ship was slightly listing to its port side. The Purser explained that likely coal had been removed from the starboard side. The excess starboard side coal consumption was most likely the result of the coal bunker fire that had been smouldering in her forward coal bunker since the end of her sea trials in Belfast. By Friday the 12 April, the Firemen or Stokers had bought the fire relatively under control.

The Marconi wireless operator, Harold Bride and John (Jack) Philips had relayed numerous messages to Captain Smith from other vessels, congratulating them and good luck on *Titanic's* maiden voyage to New York. Congratulatory messages were included from the *Empress Of Britain* and *SS. La Toutaine*. Each message had also contained warnings and advice about icebergs. The southern most location for ice came from the French liner *SS.Toutaine*, giving a latitude of 42° S, which is roughly, the Latitude of Chicago. Ice warnings in the Atlantic are not uncommon and are expected in April.

In the evening, the Marconi wireless equipment ceased to operate. Bride and Philips would work well into the night and the next morning trying to locate the problem.

As the evening and night progressed, vessels were reporting their encounters with ice all along the North Atlantic shipping lanes.

Coal Bunker Fire

As *Titanic* sank beneath the surface of the North Atlantic, many myths surfaced regarding the fire in her coal bunkers. These myths also mention different bunkers the coal was smouldering in.

The story of the coal bunker fire is true. Coal in *Titanic's* forward coal bunker No. 10 on the side of boiler room No. 6, was smouldering definitely from the time shortly after she left Southampton. Though, some testimony at the board of inquiries after the disaster, claim the fire was actually burning after she left Belfast. The coal smouldered for 4 days. No one else except the crew in the bowels of the ship knew of the coal bunker fire onboard. The passengers were enjoying the voyage of their lives. The fire continued until the smouldering coal was finally removed on April 14. As reported to Captain Smith, by Chief Engineer, Bell at 10.30am. Earlier in the day that she collided with the iceberg and the day before *Titanic* sank.

Captain Smith requested Thomas Andrews to survey the area of the coal fire, fearing the heat may have dam-

damaged the steel hull and severely compromised the watertight bulkheads. Andrews reports, the fire is extinguished but, the bulkhead that forms part of coal bunker No.10 is showing signs of heat damage.

A smouldering fire in coal bunkers onboard coal fired ships were not regarded as a hazard, they were merely regarded as a nuisance. Coal fires were not uncommon and were difficult to locate, as the base, or the seat of the smoulder might be under tons of coal. In the event of a coal fire onboard liners, it was customary to let them smoulder, until the seat of the blaze was visible, then draw the coal out from the confined space, disposing of the smouldering embers into the furnaces.

Many schools of thought exist to the present day, surrounding the coal bunker fire: when it was finally put out, which some accounts say it was on the Saturday 13 April, Some claim it was on the Sunday 14 April, another claiming the coal was still smouldering at the time *Titanic* collided with the iceberg, with the incoming water from the popped rivet seam finally extinguishing the fire. For instance, testimony at the British Inquiry from Leading Fireman, Charles Hendrickson, who joined *Titanic* at Southampton, having served previously on White Star Lines, *Oceanic*, claims: "It took us right up to the Saturday to get it out". Frederick Barrett, also claims the fire was finally put out on Saturday. Fireman J. Dilley claimed the collision with the iceberg on the Sunday 14 April finally extinguished the fire: "No, sir, we didn't get that fire out, and among the stokers there was talk, sir, that we'd have to empty the big coal bunkers after we'd put our passengers off in

New York and then call on the fireboats there to help us put out the fire."

"But we didn't need such help. It was right under bunker No. 6 that the iceberg tore the biggest hole in the *Titanic*, and the flood of water that came through, sir, put out the fire that our tons and tons of water had not been able to get rid of."

Over the decades, some publications and stories around the coal bunker fire suggests it was common knowledge among passengers and crew of *Titanic,* after she departed Southampton on April 10. Testimony from Fireman Dilly claims: "The stokers were beginning to get alarmed over it, but the officers told us to keep our mouths shut---they didn't want to alarm the passengers."

Second Officer Lightoller testified at the British Inquiry from question number 14640:

"14640. Have you at any time heard anything about a fire?"
Lightoller – "In a coal bunker?"

14641. "Yes"
Lightoller – "No."

14642. "In the ordinary course of things would a matter of that sort be reported to you as an Officer?"
Lightoller – "No, not if it was slight, or I may say unless it became serious."

14643. "Would it be reported to the Captain?"

Lightoller – "Very probably."

14644. "Whose particular duty would it be to see that any fire occurring there was put out?"
Lightoller – "The Engineer's."

2nd Officer Lightoller is claiming that he was not aware of a coal bunker fire, unless it was serious enough to warrant senior officers having their attention drawn to a problem below decks. Lightoller was the only senior Officer to survive the *Titanic* sinking, so it must be assumed the smouldering coal was never regarded as a serious threat to the vessel. It is how-ever known the ships Captain Smith was aware of the smouldering coal. But, he did not recognise it as a threat to the overall safety of the vessel under his command.

Not much information exists as to the cause of the coal bunker fire onboard *Titanic*. It is believed how-ever that Spontaneous Combustion played a major part as the cause. An interesting comment by Fireman Dilley, in a statement, said:

"The fire started in bunker No. 6. There were hundreds of tons of coal stored there. The coal on top of the bunker was wet, as all the coal should have been, but down at the bottom of the bunker the coal had been permitted to get dry."

"The dry coal at the bottom of the pile took fire, sir, and smouldered for days. The wet coal on top kept the flames from coming through, but down in the bottom of the bunker, sir, the flames was a-raging."

Contrary to Dilly's comment regarding wet and dry coal stored together. Today in the 21st Century. A website from the U.S. Department of Energy, states: "Spontaneous combustion has long been recognised as a fire hazard in stored coal. Spontaneous combustion fires usually begin as "hot spots" deep within the reserve of coal. The hot spots appear when coal absorbs oxygen from the air. Heat generated by the oxidation then initiated the fire."

In addition, a 1941 edition of *A Modern Marine Engineers Manual - Volume I*, states: "Coal should not be taken on board wet if it can be avoided, and care should be taken to keep it dry in the bunkers, as moisture sometimes causes a rapid and dangerous generation of heat and gas, which may result in spontaneous combustion. Before decks are washed down after coaling, the bunker plates should be replaced and made tight, to prevent water from getting into the bunkers."

Is it any wonder that coal bunker fires were common onboard coal fired vessels, if it were common practice to store wet and dry coal together in coal bunkers, as Fireman Dilley states?

In November 2004 Robert Essenhigh, an engineer from the Ohio State University, put forward a theory. Essenhigh claims the coal bunker fire led indirectly to the ship's collision with the iceberg. He claims a smouldering pile of coal led to the decision to gain control of the fire was to shovel more coal into the furnaces. Thus leading to *Titanic's* excessive speed in iceberg-laden waters.

Essenhigh states that records prove that fire control teams were on standby at the ports of Southampton and Cherbourg because of a fire in the stockpile, and that such fires are known to reignite after they have been supposedly extinguished. He suggests that the *Titanic* actually set off from Southampton with one of its bunkers on fire, or that a Spontaneous Combustion of coal occurred after the ship left port. Such fires were a common phenomenon aboard coal-fired ships and one of many reasons why marine transportation switched to oil in the early 1900s.

~ ~ ~ ~

Titanic covered 519 miles between noon Friday and noon Saturday 13 April.

Laurence Beesley remembered that at lunch on Sunday, many of the passengers were remarking how they were enjoying the progress of the vessel. Comparing her against the other, faster Trans-Atlantic steamers, *Titanic's* slower motion also meant far less vibration and that made this voyage the most comfortable ride they had ever experienced on any steamer between the UK and America. The faster ships often presented a screw-like motion as they bore through the waves, as distinct from *Titanic's* straight up and down motion.

Captain Smith began his daily inspection of the ship at 10.30am. During the engine room inspection, Chief Engineer Bell advised Smith that the fire in coal bunker 6 had finally been extinguished and also reported the bulkhead and coal bunkers' signs of heat damage. A fireman was ordered to rub oil over the heat damaged areas.

The coal dust and the heat in the boiler rooms was a stark contrast to the freezing temperature up on deck as hour after hour the hot, backbreaking labour down in the bowels of the ship continued.

The morning of Sunday 14 April, dawned fine, with a smooth sea and a moderate south-easterly wind. *Titanic*, however, sailed through a front later in the morning, that marked a change in the weather, with brisk northwest winds of 20 knots.

Temperatures continued to drop from a relatively mild 55° F to about 50° F by mid-day. The temperature continued to fall throughout the afternoon and into the night. By 7.30pm the temperature was down to 33° F. By 10.30pm, it had dropped to 4° F below freezing and in order to prevent subfreezing temperatures hundreds of miles at 41° N at sea, the air mass temperature was very cold.

The ship that never sank

The story of *Titanic*, though heavily laden with myths and folklore since April 1912, just would not be quite complete without the obligatory conspiracy theory.

Conspiracy theories always contain the mandatory government cover-up, the hundreds and thousands of other people involved, who for some reason do not ever come forward to reveal the truth. These people are always the co-conspirators who are sworn to secrecy. No matter how far back in history the conspiracy is supposed to exist, no one ever comes forward to reveal the dastardly scheme. For the hundreds and thousands of people involved in the original conspiracy in 1912 - over one hundred years since - there must be additional tens of thousands who are aware of the original secrets. Still, no one ever comes forward to reveal the apparent truth. Conspiracy theories are never anything more than just conjecture and unsubstantiated claims.

One such theory is that *Titanic* did not strike an iceberg and sink on April 14, 1912. According to the conspiracy, it was *RMS Olympic* that sank, leaving *Titanic* to survive and continue through to 1937, when the vessel was supposedly scrapped.

Repairs to *Olympic*, after her collision with the Royal Navy cruiser *HMS Hawke*, posed problems for White Star Line and the Olympic-Class liners owners, The International Mercantile Marine Company, owned by J P Morgan, because the specialist marine insurance company, Lloyds of London, refused to pay out for the damage received to *Olympic*.

Olympic was sent for repairs to Harland and Wolff in Belfast. The workers were sworn to secrecy and patched up the damage, knowing the vessel would, probably not survive a sailing to New York. The great plan was set in motion to switch the identity of the two ships, then set other ships in a predetermined location to rescue the passengers and crew, while the supposed new ship sank to the bottom of the ocean.

Two main theories exist as an explanation for what happened next. One theory describes a German U-Boat sinking the vessel with a torpedo, in a vein attempt to initiate World War 1. Another claims White Star Line colluded with a German U-Boat Captain to sink the ship.

Another theory suggests *Titanic* actually struck an ice field, instead of a single berg, while the other suggests she did hit an iceberg. Most conspiracy theories usually have many variations, depending on who is actually telling the story. *Titanic's* conspiracy theories are no different.

The newest theory is one authored by Robin Gardiner in 2012, suggesting *Titanic* was swapped with *Olympic* then collided with another ship, which was blacked out to hide itself, until sea valves were opened, allowing *Olympic* to sink slowly, allowing this other darkened ship and the close by *Californian* - which was also involved in the dastardly deed, under secrecy of course - to rescue all passengers and crew. But things went wrong, resulting in the loss of over 1500 passengers and crew.

Lack of evidence has nothing to do with the theories. Conspiracy theories persist without viable evidence to support the claims. No surviving passenger or crew member noticed a torpedo slamming into the side of *Titanic*. All surviving passengers and crew recounted what they were doing and where they were at the time *Titanic* struck the iceberg. Not one recounted the vessel striking another ship.

~ ~ ~ ~

Titanic had covered 546 miles between Saturday and Sunday morning. Early morning risers enjoyed a sunny stroll along the promenade and boat decks, as the peaks of water were shining like diamonds as the early morning sun shone on the surface of the ocean. Even though the breeze was chilly and invigorating, Captain Smith had planned a Lifeboat drill for all passengers and crew for that day but, because of the chilly temperature outside and so Sunday services could be conducted, he chose to delay any lifeboat drill until Monday 15 April, 1912.

Smith and Ismay had earlier discussed the possibility of increasing the ships speed to increase on Monday 15 April from a steady 21 knots to a maximum speed of 24 knots, to test her performance. Then gradually reduce the speed again to 21 knots. Both Smith and Ismay had tentatively agreed on this move prior to departing Queenstown on 11 April, they had subsequently realised that increasing the speed would place greater demands on the new engines, which could cause serious damage to the ships new engines.

Top left - First Class gymnasium, reading and writing room.
Bottom - First Class grand staircase, heated Swimming pool

Church services were conducted for the First class passengers by Captain Smith, while Father Thomas Byles conducted a Catholic Mass in the Second Class Lounge, then another Mass for the Third Class passengers. Afterwards the passengers continued to enjoy the facilities onboard the ship, such as the Reading and Writing rooms, reading in the ship's Libraries, relaxing in the sun or perhaps trying out the electric horse in the Gymnasium, or enjoying the heated swimming pool or Turkish bath. Whatever they personally chose, they were having the time of their lives. Colonel Archibald Gracie later stated:

"I enjoyed myself as if I were in a summer palace on the seashore, surrounded by every comfort".

Rev. Mr Carter, a Church Of England clergyman had asked the ship's Purser if he could use the saloon in the evening, as he wanted to hold a hymn sing-a-long. The purser had given his consent. Mr Carter spent the afternoon preparing for the 8.30pm start.

Captain Smith did hear some good news after the morning church service, during his daily inspection of the ship. He was informed by Chief Engineer Joseph Bell, that the fire in the number 6 starboard coal bunker had finally been extinguished. Coal bunker 6 had been smouldering for the past two weeks, since *Titanic's* sea trials in Belfast. Smith had been concerned about the fire and was considering the strong possibility of asking the New York Fire Department to assist in extinguishing the fire before Titanic's return voyage on April 20.

As the day wore on, *Titanic* was sailing into ice fields that were attributed to an extremely mild winter, causing large numbers of icebergs to drift off from the west coast of Greenland.

For the first time in 14.000 years, the moon was closer to Earth. Coinciding with the closest annual approach to the sun of Earth's orbit, which caused exceptionally high tides that may have resulted in a greater number of icebergs than usual, reaching the north Atlantic shipping lanes, via the Labrador currents. April 1912 was an exceptionally heavy month for icebergs, with the bergs flowing further south into the North Atlantic than in any other year on record. In fact, April 1912 held this record until 1972.

The Labrador Current is a cold current in the North Atlantic Ocean, which flows south from the Arctic Ocean, along the Labrador coast, passing around New Foundland and continuing south along the south coast of Nova Scotia. In both Spring and Winter, the Labrador current transports icebergs from the glaciers of Greenland southwards into the trans-Atlantic shipping lanes.

CHAPTER SIX

Iceberg, Right Ahead

When anyone asks how I can best describe my experience in nearly 40 years at sea, I merely say, uneventful. Of course there have been winter gales, and storms and fog and the like, but in all my experience, I have never been in any accident of any sort worth speaking about. ...... I never saw a wreck and never have been wrecked, nor was I ever in any predicament that threatened to end in disaster of any sort. You see, I am not very good material for a story.

- Captain E. J. Smith, Commander, R.M.S. Titanic

Throughout the day of 14 April 1912, *Titanic* had been receiving ice warnings from other ships in the area she was sailing into. Passengers onboard had also noticed increasing cold weather conditions throughout the afternoon.

At 09.00am, *Titanic* received the first of the ice warnings from *Caronia*, originating two days earlier. The message read: " Captain - *Titanic* - West-bound steamers report bergs, growlers and field ice in 42° N from 49° to 50° W, April 12th. Compliments, Barr."

Captain Smith acknowledged he had received the warning in the early afternoon at 1.42 pm, and posted it for his officers to read. Smith also received a warning that had been relayed via *RMS Baltic*, from the Greek ship *Athenia* that she was passing ice bergs and large quantities of field ice. This message read: "Greek steamer *Athenia* reports passing icebergs and large quantities of field ice, today in latitude 41° 52' W. Wish you and *Titanic* all success. Commander", this warning was also acknowledged by Smith. Smith also reported the previous warning to the chairman of White Star Line, J. Bruce Ismay and ordered a new course, which would take the ship further south, hopefully away from the ice danger.

Another ice warning, never reached Smith and the other officers on the ships bridge. This warning was from the German ship *SS Amerika*, reporting they had just "passed two large ice bergs". The *SS Amerika* was just south of *Titanic's* position at the time, the full message read: "*Amerika* passed two large icebergs at 41°

27° N, 50° 8' W on April 14". The reason why this message never reached Smith is unknown.

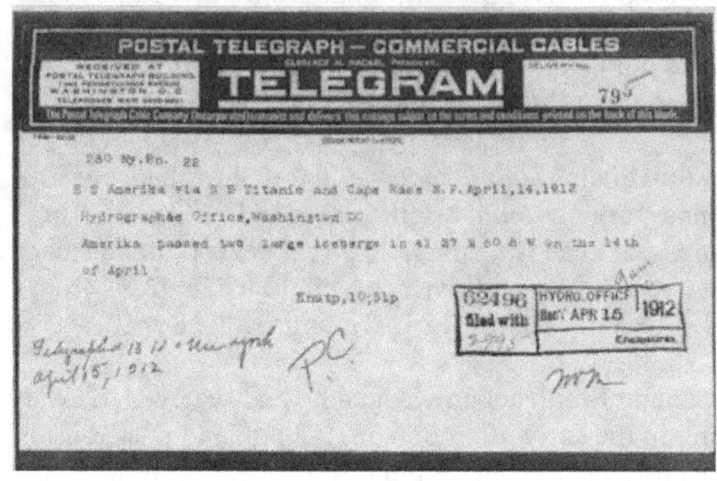

Ice warning Telegram from SS Amerika to RMS Titanic, April 14, 1912

Radio operator Jack Philips was preoccupied with transmitting passenger messages via the relay station at Cape Race, New Foundland. *Titanic's* radio equipment had broken down the day before. Although the radio set had been repaired by the morning of the 14th, the breakdown had caused a backlog of messages from passengers waiting to be sent.

First Officer Murdoch excused himself from the bridge for dinner at 6.30pm. The air temperature had dramatically dropped by 6.00pm. As day had begun to turn to night, Murdoch relieved Second Officer Lightoller at 7.05pm for his dinner break. Upon his return to the bridge at 7.35pm, Murdoch commented to Lightoller the air temperature had dropped four degrees within the last half hour, from 43° to 39° F, or 6.0° to 3.8° C.

At 7.30pm, three messages, warning of ice were intercepted from the *Californian,* which read: "to Captain *Antillian* Six-thirty pm, apparent ships time; latitude 42° 3' N longitude 49° 9 W. Three large bergs 5 miles to the southward of us. Regards, Lord". Indicating the massive ice field was then only 50 miles ahead. The message was clearly indicating the magnitude of the hazard *Titanic* was approaching.

> HON. WM. ALDEN SMITH,
> Washington, D. C.
> DEAR SIR: I have given you my observations and experiences after the disaster, but want to tell you of what occurred on Sunday night, April 14. My brother, his wife, and myself went to the cafe for dinner at about 7:15 p.m. (ship's time). When we entered there was a dinner party already dining, consisting of perhaps a dozen men and three women. Cap't Smith was a guest, as also were Mr. and Mrs, Widener, Mr. and Mrs. Blair (Thayer), and Maj. Butt, Capt. Smith was continuously with his party from the time we entered until between 9:25 and 9:45, when he bid the women good night and left. I know this time positively, for at 9:25 my brother suggested my going to bed. We waited for one more piece of the orchestra, and it was between 9:25 and 9:45 (the time we departed), that Capt. Smith left.
> Sitting within a few feet of this party were also Sir Cosmo and Lady Duff-Gordon, a Mrs. Meyers, of New York, and Mrs. Smith, of Virginia. Mr. and Mrs. Harris also were dining in the cafe at the same time.
> I had read testimony before your committee stating that Capt. Smith had talked to an officer on the bridge from 8:45 to 9:25. This is positively untrue, as he was having coffee with these people during this time. I was seated so close to them that I could hear bits of their conversation.
> Yours,
> DAISY MINAHAN.

Affidavit provided by First-Class passenger, Daisy Minahan to the U.S Senate Inquiry in the Titanic sinking.

Captain Smith was attending a dinner party in the Parisian café with Major Butt, Mr & Mrs Thayer and Mr & Mrs Widener until 9.45pm, according to an affidavit presented to the U.S. Senate Inquiry from First-Class passenger Daisy Minahan,

The night of the 14th was perfect, with no wind, the sea was flat calm, with no cloud in the sky and the stars were rising and setting with brilliant clarity.

All in all, the ice warning messages received by *Titanic* indicated a huge ice field 78 miles long, only 50 miles ahead of *Titanic* and directly in her path.

Quartermaster Robert Hitchens arrived on the bridge at 8.00pm to begin his watch. At 8.45pm, Lightoller had sent Hitchens word to the ships carpenter to drain off the fresh water tanks to prevent the pipes from freezing.

Rev. Mr Clark began his hymn sing-a-long in the saloon at 8.30pm. Welcoming all who attended, and asking them personally to choose the hymns. Mr Clark could only facilitate requests that were for the best-known, favourite hymns, while providing an explanation of each one and the circumstances in which they were composed, impressing many who attended with his knowledge and eagerness to tell the story behind each hymn.

The temperature by this time had dropped to 33° F, or minus .5° C. During the course of the last two hours, the temperature had dropped 10 degree Fahrenheit or 12.2 degrees Celsius. Captain Smith appeared on the deck at about 9.55pm, where he and 2nd Officer Lightoller discussed the unusually calm and clear conditions. Lightoller had commented to Smith about the temperature drop and reported, he had sent the carpenter to check the water tanks. In the process of discussing the unusual weather conditions, mention was made that the lack of both wind and water ripples, indicated the presence of icebergs. They both agreed that spotting icebergs would be easy because there would be a fair amount of light reflecting off them, producing an outline from quite a distance away. Lightoller and Smith did not talk about the speed of the ship.

Lightoller asked Sixth Officer Moody to ring and caution the Lookouts, that spotting bergs would be difficult under these conditions and to look carefully for ice and growlers, in particular until morning. Lightoller believed any iceberg would be spotted up to two miles away in such perfect weather conditions, despite the lack of any water ripples around the base, due to the lack of wind or swell.

Growlers were described by Lightoller at the British Board Of Trade Inquiry as: "A growler is really the worst form of ice. It is a larger berg melted down, or I might say, a solid body of ice, which is lower down to the water and more difficult to see than field ice, pack ice, floe ice, or icebergs". Put another way, a growler stands lower than an iceberg, but with equal size under water.

For the remainder of his watch, Lightoller stood, keeping an extra set of eyes, keeping a sharp lookout toward the front of the ship from the Bridge. Lightoller later testified at the Board of Trade inquiry that he was using binoculars during this time, but he mentioned that detecting icebergs was not usually possible with binoculars alone.

To question number 13688. "And you were using the glasses?" Lightoller replied "Occasionally I would raise the glasses to my eyes and look ahead to see if I could see anything, using both glasses and my eyes."

To question number, 13690, the solicitor general asked Lightoller to clarify his answer, by asking: "You see, Mr. Lightoller, I want to get your own view. You will tell us candidly and fairly, I am sure. First of all, in your own experience, when you have used glasses, have you in fact found ice with the help of glasses?". Lightoller replied: "Never. I have never seen ice through glasses first, never in my experience. Always whenever I have seen a berg, I have seen it first with my eyes and then examined it through glasses", meaning, to be able to spot an iceberg, you must first have a point of reference to be able to view the object.

At 10.00pm, the temperature had dropped by another one degree to 32° F or 0° C, which is the freezing point of fresh water.

Second Officer Lightoller was relieved on the bridge by 1st Officer Murdoch, who was wearing his overcoat as he came onto the bridge, commenting on the freezing temperature.

In the ordinary process of handing over a ship, Lightoller mentioned to Murdoch, the ship was steering by standard compass. They both commented on the Marconi-grams that mentioned ice. They both knew they had entered the ice region. Lightoller mentioned to Murdoch that he had issued a warning to the crows-nest. Quartermaster Hitchens was given his course of

N. 71° W. sailing the same course Quartermaster Olliver was given at 6.00pm. Also on the bridge at that time were Fourth Officer Boxhall and Sixth Officer Moody. At the same time, Frederick Fleet and Reginald Lee were relayed instructions for the night, while relieving Archie Jewell and George Symons on the Crows-Nest.

The final warning came in from, the *Californian* at 11.00pm stating: "we are stopped and surrounded by ice", 19 miles away from Titanic's position. Cyril Evans from *Californian* received a sharp reply from *Titanic* radio operator Philips "Keep out! Shut up! You are jamming my signal. I am working Cape Race".

On Sunday, 14 April, 1912, the night was clear, calm and very cold. The sea was, as Second Class passenger, Lawrence Beesley would later recount, "like a millpond". *Titanic* was sailing at 21 knots as was standard practice in 1912. Although *Titanic* had previously received a total of six reports warning of ice. Captain Smith had previously stated he could not "imagine any condition which would cause a ship to founder. Modern shipbuilding has gone beyond that".

Before turning in for the night, Lightoller inspected the decks to ensure everything was all right. After completing that duty, known as 'Going Round' Lightoller returned to the bridge before going to his cabin. Smith issued the usual order to rouse him, "if it becomes at all doubtful, let me know. I will be just inside' Smith retired for the night at 10.25pm. Second Officer Lightoller also retired to his cabin. After getting into his bed and turning off the light, Lightoller lay awake.

The hymn sing-a-long in the saloon, hosted by Rev. Mr Clark was drawing to an end by 10.30pm, as the stewards were waiting to serve coffee and biscuits, before going off duty for the night. Throughout the meeting, many hymns were requested that dealt with dangers at sea and the last hymn sung was *"For Those In Peril On The Sea"*. No person who attended the hymn meeting, or those whiling away the night time hours on *Titanic*, had any indication that the real peril on the sea lay only a few nautical miles ahead.

No Binoculars

At 11.40pm, *Titanic* was still cruising through the ocean at 21 knots. From the crow's-nest, Frederick Fleet and Reginald Lee were finding it hard to see the horizon, or much of anything else, because of the effects of the freezing air against their naked eyes and the refraction of the light.

Lee would testify that glasses or binoculars were not generally provided for the crows-nest. A question from the Attorney-General - number 2367 - asked: "Are glasses usually supplied to the Lookout man on Mail steamers?" Lee would reply: 'Not that I know". It must be remembered, Lee had previously had 16 years experience at sea.

Fleet and Lee would testify at the British Board of Trade inquiry, there was a slight haze on the waterline, all around *Titanic* along the Horizon, from about 11.00pm.

Suddenly Fleet noticed a slightly blurred, black object slowly appearing from the haze, like a dark hole against the moonless sky and rang the look-out bell three times. Then alerted Moody on the bridge of an "iceberg, right ahead."

Later, Fleet testified about what he saw from the Look-out: " I have no idea of distances or spaces. It kept getting larger as we were getting nearer it."

It remains debatable, if Fleet and Lee had had the use of binoculars, whether or not they would have benefitted from them, in detecting an iceberg in such conditions. To use binoculars, to view an object up-close, you have to determine a point of reference first. As previously mentioned, the weather conditions were freezing. Such cold and hazy conditions will make an iceberg look dark, as there will not be present any light to illuminate such an object. Lookouts Fleet and Lee were trying to differentiate a dark object against a backdrop of black surroundings. To use binoculars would have been useless as they would not be able to determine any point of reference. This could explain Frederick Fleet's later comment about not being able to determine distance and space.

The Second Officer for *Titanic's* voyage from the place of her birth, Belfast to Southampton - David Blair - was replaced on April 9, for preference from Captain Smith of Henry Wilde.

Wilde was promoted to First Officer, with Murdoch. Second Officer, Charles Lightoller occupied Blairs Cabin for *Titanic's* maiden voyage, unaware that Blair, when leaving the ship in Southampton, had unintentionally removed the key to the locker, containing the lookout binoculars. As lookout binoculars were not generally supplied by shipping lines, it was most probably not realised, White Star had supplied them for *Titanic*.

~ ~ ~ ~

At that moment, First Class passenger George Brayton was on the Promenade deck and heard the warning come from the ships lookout. "A number of us who were enjoyed the crisp air were promenading about the deck. Captain Smith was on the bridge when the first cry from the lookout came that there was an iceberg ahead. It may have been 30 feet high when I saw it. It was possibly 200 yards away and dead ahead. Captain Smith shouted some orders. A number of us promenaders rushed to the bow of the ship. When we saw she could not fail to hit it, we rushed to the stern. Then came a crash, and the passengers were panic-stricken."

6th Officer Moody acknowledges with a simple "thank you" to the message from the Look-out, then repeats "iceberg, right ahead" to First Officer William Murdoch, who immediately ordered the ship - according to testimony from Quartermaster Robert Hitchens, " Hard-a-starboard" - Hard-a-Starboard is a tiller command, meaning, turn the Tiller to the starboard and the ship will turn to the Port. Murdoch, then set the telegraph to "Full Astern. Stop".

Quartermaster Alfred Olliver walked onto the bridge at the moment of half collision and ordered the ship to "Hard-a-Port". The ship will turn to the Starboard. This manoeuvre is known as, "Port Around" and explains why *Titanic's* stern was not damaged in the collision. It also explains Murdoch's comment to Captain Smith, about 5 minutes after the collision, when Smith entered the bridge, "I intended to port around it."

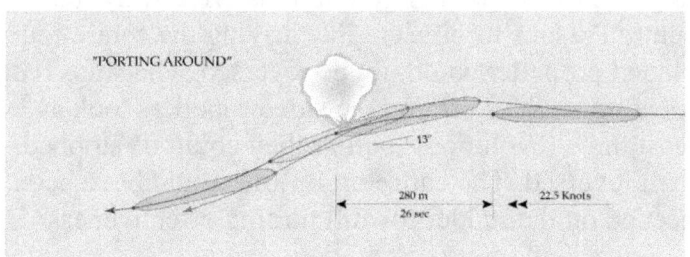

Titanic's course at the time of collision

Quartermaster Hitchens later testified that turning the wheel hard right, did nothing to prevent the ship hitting the iceberg: "But, during the time, she was crushing the ice, or we could hear the grinding noise along the ship's bottom. I heard the telegraph ring, sir. The skipper came rushing out of his room - Captain Smith - and asked, "What is that" Mr. Murdoch said: "iceberg." He - Captain Smith – said: "Close the emergency doors"… Mr. Murdoch replied: "The doors are already closed."

It's worth noting here that a ship's tiller is the mechanism that turns the ships rudder. As is with larger ships, the bigger the ship, the greater the force needed to turn the rudder. A ships tiller is attached to the Rudder post or Rudder stock and provides the torque for the helmsman to turn the rudder with the ships wheel. In larger ships, the tiller turns in the opposite direction the ship is intended to turn. It is not known if First Officer William Murdoch actually ordered the tiller turned to Starboard, as was interpreted, or if his intention was for the ship to turn to starboard in an attempt to avoid the iceberg.

The ships rudder was adequate - 30 m² or 280 square feet to move a mass of 46,000 tons effectively, but the centre Parsons turbine engine, driving the centre four bladed propeller could not be reversed. The ships reciprocating engines driving the side propellers took at least three revolutions, before they could be stopped, then reversed. The entire prop flow would have been needed on the rudder for full turning effectiveness.

Lee described what they saw, as the ship was approaching the iceberg, after it had been spotted by himself and Fleet: "Can you give us any idea of the breadth? What did it look like? It was something that was above the forecastle?" To which Lee replied "It was a dark mass that came through that haze, there was no white appearing, until it was just close alongside the ship, that was just the fringe at the top". Lee continues: "Through the haze, and as she moved away from it, there was just a white fringe along the top. That was the only white about it. Until she passed by, then you could see she was white; one side of it seemed to be black, and the other side seemed to be white."

The haze, an optical illusion

Throughout the day on 14 April 1912, *Titanic* was traveling through an Arctic High, presenting the highest pressure anywhere in the Northern hemisphere at that time. The high pressure was from a warm Gulf Stream air flow, above *Titanic's* position. At the time of her sinking, *Titanic* was at about the centre of the high pressure area. The water temperature was freezing, creating an extremely cold air temperature around *Titanic*, extending upwards to the level of the warmer air current. The air between the water surface and the warmer air was condensed around the ship.

April of 1912 saw an unusually large amount of Ice and Ice bergs in the shipping lanes of the North Atlantic. Usually there are about 500 icebergs at that time of the year. But April 1912, saw in excess of 1000 icebergs, carried from the West coast of Greenland, extending south to the southern most track for Trans-Atlantic shipping, carried by the Labrador Current. The Labrador Current brings the bergs and the colder water south, under the warmer Gulf Stream current.

At the time, in the early years of weather forecasting, Trans-Atlantic shipping took water temperatures every four hours and recorded each temperature reading. These temperatures were recorded for the US and UK weather services.

On April 14th, earlier in the day *Titanic* would founder, the *Paula*, was most likely the last ship to cross the same area *Titanic* would later sink, recorded water temperatures to be changing from 12.8° C to minus 1.4 to minus 13°, with "much refraction". On the 13th April, in the same position, the German steamer *Deutchland*, recorded "Much refraction on the horizon". After leaving New York on April 11th, the steamer, *Marengo*, while steaming near the position on April 14th, recorded the sea temperature dropping dramatically with "Much refraction on a clear, bright night."

Refraction, is a distortion of visible light. Similar to the mirage effect you will see in a desert or on a road surface on a hot day. A mirage is caused by the light distorting upwards and creating a reflected image of the blue sky onto the hot surface, giving the impression of water on the hot surface.

Refraction described here is the distortion of light, downwards, creating a mirage of the water surface onto the warmer air above the water surface, thus creating a false horizon. Put another way, this type of refraction causes the horizon to appear to be considerably higher than it actually is. This illusion is known by mariners as, Fata Morgana. An unusual name being taken from Fata - a Latin name meaning "fairy" and Morgana, taken from the name of the sorceress in the tale of King Arthur.

A "Fata Morgana" was believed to be an illusion created by witchcraft, to amaze and lure sailors to their deaths. The visible horizon could be many metres above the actual horizon, making the visible horizon at night-time look hazy and at the same time, similar to a mirage or even a rainbow. No matter how far you travel towards the optical illusion, or haze, you will never actually reach it.

Fata Morgana can give the illusion that an object on the horizon is up-side down, with a stretched zone above the horizon. It can also make an object look as if it is floating in the air above the water, as the light distorts the object. It can also make a large vessel, such as *Titanic*, look smaller on the horizon as the visible horizon obscures the lower portion of the ship, in doing so, hiding the actual length of the ship. The crew onboard *Californian* may not have been dishonest when they said that the ship on the horizon did not look big enough to be *Titanic*.

During the daylight, a Fata Morgana can also look similar to a wall of water on the horizon. At night, under moonless conditions, it would look as if there were a haze on the horizon.

Fata Morgana, taken from the Pacific Coast of the U.S. It is easy to see how the very top outline of this illusion can be recognized as an horizon on a cold, dark moonless light.

In clear conditions, it was generally believed an iceberg would be spotted about 20 minutes away, or about a mile and a half to two miles away. Fata Morgana or the false horizon would have made the approaching iceberg appear invisible, until it was too late. In fact, right up until only 37 seconds before colliding with *Titanic*.

~ ~ ~ ~

37 seconds after the iceberg had been sighted by Frederick Fleet, *Titanic*'s Bow side swiped with the berg, scraped and ground along 300m from the starboard bow, buckled her hull in several places, caused rivets to pop, created a series of holes below the waterline, while opening up her first five compartments to the sea.

An engine room greaser, Alfred White would later testify:

"I was on the whale deck, in the bow, calling the watch that was to relieve when the ice first came aboard. The collision opened the seams below the water-line but did not even scratch the paint above the line. I know that, because I was one of those who helped to make an examination over the side with a lantern. I went down into the engine-room at 12:40am. We even made coffee, so there was not much thought of danger. An hour later I was still working at the light engines. I heard the chief engineer tell one of his subordinates that number six bulkhead had given way. At that time things began to look bad…"

In the wheelhouse, immediately behind the bridge, Quartermaster Hitchens was in darkness, except for the glow of light from the ships compass, and so could not see the approaching iceberg, but "felt the ship tremble, and I felt rather a grinding nature along the ships bottom". Boxhall entered the bridge shortly after the collision and saw that Murdoch, Moody and the Captain were all together on the bridge. Boxhall witnessed the discussion between Smith and Murdoch: "The Captain said "What have we struck? Mr Murdoch said "We have struck an iceberg". Mr Murdoch continued "I put her hard a starboard and ran the engines full astern. But, it was too late; she hit it" Then Murdoch said; "I intended to port around it". Boxhall, Murdoch and Smith then looked over the starboard side of the bridge and observed, what Boxhall described as a black mass, protruding out of the water about 30 feet high toward, the stern of the ship.

Two photos of the same iceberg, providing evidence of the berg that is believed to have sunk Titanic. The top photo was taken by the Chief Steward of the German ocean liner SS Prinz Adalbert on April 15 1912, as they sailed near the site where Titanic sank the night before. He had noticed a streak of anti-fouling red paint near the icebergs base. The bottom photo was taken by Captain De Carteret of the cable ship, Minia, after being sent to the scene of the sinking to recover corpses. The red paint and scrape gouges on the bottom photo are clearly visible, indicating a large ship had struck the iceberg.

Fireman George Beauchamp was situated in the No 10 Stokehold, second from the Bow. At the British Board of Trade Inquiry he described the impact as "Just like thunder, the roar of thunder". Beauchamp later testified the only order after the collision was from the telegraph to "Stop."

First fireman Fred Barrett - in Boiler Room 6 - first to the bow ordered the dampers shut, as he heard a gushing noise of water coming into the Boiler Room. As the watertight doors were closing, he escaped into the adjoining Boiler Room 5 astern, which was also damaged slightly. A few minutes after the ship stopped, the watertight doors were closing. As the water was entering through the damaged portions of plating, the firemen continued to "Draw the fires". Fifteen minutes later, the fires were drawn, the firemen escaped up the escape ladders, Fireman Beauchamp made his way to the boat deck.

Governess Elizabeth Shutes - sitting in her First Class cabin felt a shudder reverberate throughout the ship. "Suddenly, a queer quivering ran under me, apparently the whole length of the ship. Startled by the very strangeness of the shivering motion, I sprang to the floor. With too perfect a trust in that mighty vessel, I again lay down. Some one knocked at my door, and the voice of a friend said: 'Come quickly to my cabin; an iceberg has just passed our window; I know we have just struck one."

Captain Smith ordered Boxhall to check the seaworthiness of the vessel. Boxhall went as far below as the lowest passenger deck, and the furthest forward as possible. He returned to the bridge, informing Smith he could not find any evidence of damage. Still being unsure, Smith ordered Boxhall to find the carpenter and sound the vessel. Boxhall wasn't far from the bridge when the ships carpenter brushed past him, explaining to Smith "The ship is making water". Closely followed by Postal clerk Jago Smith, reporting: "the post office is flooded to the ceiling".

J. Bruce Ismay, who had felt a tremble that awoke him in his suite on B-Deck, could not get an answer to what had happened from a steward. Ismay then made his way to the bridge and asked Captain Smith, "what happened?" Smith replied "we struck ice". Ismay then asked if Smith believed the damage was serious and Smith said that he thought it was. Ismay then left the bridge, running into Chief Engineer Bell, who informed him, the damage was serious, but he believed that the pumps would be able to control the incoming water.

The Carpenter joined with designer, Thomas Andrews, to inspect the ship further. Just after midnight on 15 April, Andrews reported back to the Captain with the bad news.

The ships situation was: Water in the forepeak - water in hatch No 1 and No 2 - Water in the Post Office - Water in Boiler Room No 6. Water 4.20 metres above the keel in the first five compartments. Within the next ten minutes, the pumps would not be able to control the inrush of water. Andrews continued to explain: The

Bulkheads between the fifth and the sixth did not go any further than E-Deck. The weight of the inrushing water would lower the ships bow, allowing the water to flood compartment No 6 from above, then continue to flood No 7 and so on. There was no way out. Wilding had calculated, the holes punched into the hull must be ridiculously small.

Andrews continued by estimating *Titanic* will founder in one hour, two hours at most. Smith was horrified at the news. He proceeded to the Marconi wireless room and instructed Bride and Philips to use the CQD distress signal, including we are going down at the head. Come quick. Immediate assistance required.

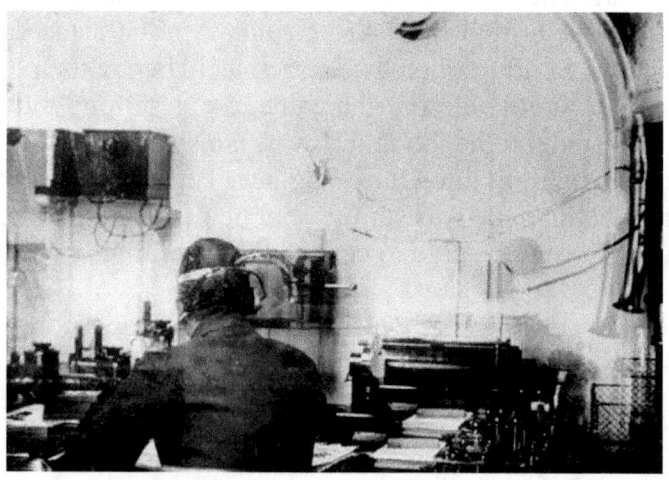

The only known photograph of the Titanic Marconi Wireless Room. Taken by Father Browne who boarded Titanic at Southampton on 10 April 1912, leaving the ship at Queenstown, Southern Ireland on 11 April 1912

The CQD was adopted for radio use in 1904. For land morse code lines, the CQ was used to identify precautionary or alert messages of interest to all stations along the telegraph line. CQ was also adopted as a "general call" for maritime radio use. How-ever, with land based systems, there was no recognised general emergency call, so the Marconi Company introduced the "D", meaning, "Distress", to CQ. Meaning, "General Call, Distress". As opposed to the popular belief that CQD means "Come Quick, Distress or "Come Quick, Danger etc. Such interpretations are simply false.

CQD of − · − ·   − − · −   − · · was used worldwide by Marconi operators. But, was never recognised as an international standard distress call, as in areas of poor reception, it could easily be confused as a "General Call". At the second International Radiographic Convention, held in Berlin, Germany in 1906. Germany's Notzeichen distress signal of three-dots/three-dashes/three-dots, · · · − − − · · ·. Or, SOS was adopted as the Internationally standard distress signal. Titanic's wireless operators used a mix of the CQD and SOS signals.

Fourth Officer Boxhall had dead reckoned the ship's position as being at latitude 41° 46' N and longitude 50° 14' W, which he then handed to the Marconi wireless operator for immediate transmission. Unfortunately, Boxhall's 'dead reckoning' had placed *Titanic* 13 nautical miles East of the ship's true position.

Harold Cottam, Wireless operator on the Cunard Liner, *Carpathia*, enroute from New York to Fiume, Austria-Hungary, via Liverpool, Genoa, Naples and Trieste, had been aware that *Titanic* chief wireless operator Philips had had a busy day. Earlier he had been listening to messages from Cape Race, intended for *Titanic*. Before he retired and went to bed, Cottam decided to contact Philips and enquire if he had received the earlier messages. "Good morning, old man - GM OM _. Do you know there are messages for you at Cape Race?". The reply from Philips was alarming, he felt his blood run cold, "CQD…CQD…MGY. Come at once. We have struck a berg. It's a CQD, old man - CQD OM - Position 41.46 N, 50.14 W."

Cottam was stunned for a few moments, then asked if he should inform the Captain. Philips replied immediately with "Yes, quick". Cottam ran to the bridge and informed First officer Dean, who did not hesitate. He immediately descended the ladder, through the chartroom and entered the Captains cabin, with Cottam following. An anxious Dean explained the message from *Titanic*. Captain Rostron immediately swung into action, saying "Mr. Dean, turn the ship around-steer northwest, I'll work out the course for you in a minute". Dean rushed back to the bridge. Rostron turned to Cottam, "Are you sure it's the *Titanic* and she requires immediate assistance?" Cottam replied "Yes Sir", Rostron asked "You are absolutely certain?" Cottam replied "Quite certain, sir". Captain Rostron then said "All right, tell him we are coming along as fast as we can."

At about this time, ten miles NNW of *Titanic*'s actual position, the tramp-steamer, *Californian* was surrounded by ice and stopped for the night. At 12.15pm, Third Officer Groves had entered the wireless room and asked wireless operator Cyril Evans if he were in contact with anyone interesting, if he had any news.

Evans replied, "I think the *'Titanic'* is near us. I have got her". He continued, "You know, the new boat on its maiden voyage."

But after an earlier snarling from *Titanic* wireless operator, Philips, at 11.35pm he had decided he has had enough and was retiring for the night after turning off his wireless set. Before leaving the *Californians* wireless room, Groves had picked up the headset and put them on, as he was quite interested in wireless equipment, and was quite good at reading messages. But he was not familiar with *Californians* equipment. *Californian's* station had a magnetic detector, which required winding up. Groves did not wind it up, so was unable to hear anything. He put the headset down, sighed and walked away.

Sea water began filling the forward compartments Of *Titanic*, while spilling over into other compartments. With more than four of her compartments open to the Atlantic Ocean, *Titanic,* was doomed.

CHAPTER SEVEN

Women And Children First

Icebergs loomed up and fell astern and we never slackened. It was an anxious time with the Titanic's fateful experience very close in our minds. There were 700 souls on Carpathia and those lives as well as the survivors of the Titanic herself depended on the sudden turn of the wheel.

- Captain Arthur H. Rostron, Commander, Carpathia

With his 40 years experience at sea, Smith knew the importance of a calm and orderly evacuation, and with the information he had received, the fate of his ship. He was perfectly aware of the ratio of passengers aboard and the lack of lifeboats. Yet, on the night of the 14th April 1912, he never gave an order to Abandon Ship. Twenty minutes after the ship's collision with the iceberg, Smith gave the order to "Prepare the Lifeboats", and also ordered the passengers and crew to put their lifebelts on.

The long held belief - certainly held by *Carpathia's* Captain, was that *Titanic* lay 58 nautical miles away to the South-East. The discovery of the wreck site of *Titanic* in 1985, proved that the actual distance was 47 nautical miles. Captain Rostron of *RMS Carpathia* had never before, in his career had to respond to a CQD or SOS from any other vessel. The CQD from *Titanic* was a clear call to duty.

As he rushed into the ships chart room, he kept calm, as he was aware there were no room for hesitation, no second-guessing - he had to provide the assistance.

 Having first worked out his new course over the chart table, Rostron ascended the ladder to the bridge and gave the helmsman the new course-North 52 West. Rostron next telegraphed the engine room "Full Speed Ahead". He knew that to cover the distance between them and *Titanic* would take four hours at *Carpathia's* top speed of 14 knots - He was totally unaware the actual distance to the stricken *Titanic* would take far less travel time at 14 knots. Rostron next called out all off duty stokers and off duty watch, to get as much speed as possible from the engines. Rostron also ordered the heating to be cut off from crew and passenger accommodations, to make every ounce of steam the boilers made to go into the engines.

Rostron then gave a series of orders to First officer Dean to prepare all lifeboats and swing them over the side, in preparation for a major rescue operation, for strings of lights to be hung along the sides of the ship, all gangway doors to be opened, slings made ready for hoisting injured survivors aboard, for cargo netting to be slung over the side for survivors to climb aboard, for canvas bags to be made available for lifting small children aboard and for oil bags to be prepared for pouring on rough seas, if required.

Rostron next called for the ships surgeon, Dr. McGee and two other passenger surgeons, and assigned each man to take charge of one of three first aid stations. McGee was assigned to the First Class station, the Italian doctor was assigned to the Second Class station and the Hungarian doctor was assigned to the Third Class station, with each station being set up in the dining room of each class. Stewards and pursers were assigned to cover respective gangways. As survivors boarded, they took note of names and class, then ensured they are directed to their respective first aid stations. Coffee and whiskey would also be provided. The smoking room, library and lounge were all converted into dormitories. *Carpathia's* Third Class passengers were also grouped together to make more room for Third Class survivors. Stewards were stationed along the corridors to prevent the inevitable 'curious' passengers from getting in the way of rescue efforts.

Titanic was attempting a speed record

Rumours originating from American press reports of 1912 suggest that *Titanic's* maiden voyage was used by White Star Line, not only to display the splendour of their newest vessel, portraying *Titanic* as not exclusive of the only vessel of opulent magnificence and size, but to also display her speed capabilities.

White Star Line Chief Executive J. Bruce Ismay is believed to have persuaded Captain Smith - thus being accused of interfering with the navigation of his ship, to attempt to win the prestigious Blue Riband. An award presented for the fastest Trans-Atlantic voyage from Southampton to New York, thus explaining the reason why *Titanic* did not slow down before striking the iceberg.

The Blue Riband was an unofficial accolade or 'Gentleman's agreement' - awarded to regular passenger vessels sailing the Westbound route of the North Atlantic, against the Gulf Stream current. Twenty five British vessels have been awarded the mythical Blue Riband, throughout maritime history from 1830. Five of those vessels were owned by White Star Line, thirteen were owned by the Cunard Line. The accolade was awarded to White Star Line's *Adriatic* in 1872, *Germanic* in 1877, *Majestic* and *Teutonic* in 1891. Cunard Line's *Lusitania* first achieved the Blue Riband honours in October 1907, beating her own record again in May 1908, July 1908 and August 1909 with the highest average speed of 25.65 knots, until the *Mauritania* outpaced *Lusitania* in September 1909, with a top average speed of 26.06 knots.

In 1935, the Blue Riband trophy became official, after a British politician and owner of Hale's Brothers Shipping Company, Harold K. Hales donated the prize, which was named the 'Hale's Trophy'. The rules related to the unofficial accolade were changed to any commercial surface vessel crossing the North Atlantic in either direction.

The Blue Riband was, in 1912 an unofficial prize for the fastest crossing of the North Atlantic. It's quite ironic that a mythical Trans-Atlantic prize would be associated with *Titanic,* given that *Titanic* was traveling the extreme Southern route to New York to avoid, what Captain Smith recognised was an extended ice field, which actually extended a lot farther south than his intended southern route. While Smith's intended southern route was believed to be southern enough to avoid ice fields for the month of April. A speed record attempt would have been along the northern route, being the shortest distance between Europe and America.

Cunard Lines *Lusitania* and *Mauritania* were built for speed and both vessels could achieve speeds in excess of 26 knots as opposed to *Titanic's* 24 knots. *Titanic* was no match as a viable competitor against *Lusitania* and *Mauritania* because *Titanic* was designed and built for luxury and safety above speed.

~ ~ ~ ~

Carpathia was sailing towards the coordinates provided by Chief wireless operator Philips on *Titanic*.

Meanwhile, Captain Rostron re-assessed all his orders and concluded he had done all he could in preparing his ship to assist *Titanic*. His next concern was to do what he could to ensure that *Carpathia* did not meet the same fate as the stricken vessel. To that end, he posted extra lookouts in strategic positions such as the bow forecastle and ships bridge.

Titanic's crew had not been adequately trained in evacuation procedures in the event of a serious mishap at sea. The evidence presented to the later US and British inquiries also showed, all too painfully, the total inadequacy of the Officers in respect of their knowledge of the procedure for firing distress rockets and in which order. The crew did not know which boats they would be stationed at during an evacuation at sea and the Officers did not know how many passengers could be accommodated in the lifeboats prior to launching.

Although all twenty of her life boats were launched, most were launched into the cold Atlantic barely half full and Lifeboat number 1, was occupied by only twelve people from the starboard side. As previously stated, most were launched only half full but the last few were launched over-full, with some survivors claiming the water was up to the rim.

Thirty minutes after the collision - at 12.05am - the ship was taking a noticeable dip in the ocean at the Bow, the squash court, 32 feet or 9.7 m above the level of the keel was flooding.

Many First Class passengers appeared on deck in bed clothes, covered only with coats, yet the lifeboats were only beginning to be uncovered as the ships band, under the leadership of Wallace Hartley, were playing a medley of cheerful ragtime tunes to "Keep the spirits up" of those who were beginning to wonder if something might be wrong. Some passengers thought that the entire procedure was unnecessary. A deafening roar emulated throughout all the decks as coal stokers drew out the fires, relieving pressure from the boilers to prevent an explosion from the cold seawater rushing into the bowels of the ship.

As the first lifeboat was being launched at 12.45am, a sudden whoosh emulated out as the first rocket shot 800 feet into the night sky above *Titanic*, fired from the bridge by Fourth Officer Boxhall. Lighting the night sky above *Titanic* and amusing young children with its 12 brilliant white stars slowly floating down, as their parents were trying to get them aboard the lifeboats.

Lifeboats

Titanic's lifeboats play a major part in the Folklore surrounding the disaster. It is well known that *Titanic's* 20 lifeboats could only cater for 1,178 passengers and crew. On her maiden voyage, *Titanic* was carrying 2.223 people from Southampton to New York, although *Titanic* was designed to carry up to 3,300 people.

In 1912, the tradition for loading lifeboats during an emergency was" Women and children first". This tradition often caused time delays in filling the lifeboats as the women and children were singled out for priority in lifeboat placement, which often led to lifeboats being launched half full. This was certainly the case with *Titanic*.

A great number of passengers - believing the activity on the boat deck was nothing more than a lifeboat drill - preferred the warmth inside the ship, rather than the cold air outside. Captain Smith also never gave the order to Abandon Ship, which led to a belief among the majority of the passengers, they were in no particular danger. These time delays resulted in the first lifeboat leaving the ship at 12.45am - over a full hour after the ships collision with the iceberg and 40 minutes after Captain Smith ordered the lifeboats to be prepared. The port side lifeboats were mainly filled with women and children and a few men. However, on the starboard side, men, women and children were loaded prior to launching into the cold Atlantic Ocean.

The first lifeboat launched from the starboard side of the ship contained only 12 people. The majority, were launched half full and did not return to *Titanic* to pick up drowning victims, due to passenger and crew concerns of swamping the boats. Two did return to pick up other victims, but the majority of them died before *RMS Carpathia* arrived at 4am, two hours after *Titanic* sunk. The rescue continued until the last lifeboat was collected at 8.30am.

The lack of lifeboats was the result of outdated maritime regulations. The Merchant Shipping Act of 1884 stipulated the number of lifeboats for a vessel up to 10,000 tons. By 1912, this limit had been exceeded by the growth in size of newer vessels. *Titanic's* gross registered tonnage was 46,328 tons. This was not uncommon at the time, and the White Star Line believed its new Olympic-class ships could remain afloat until the passengers and crew were transferred to a rescue vessel.

This common belief is perfectly outlined and explained by the Captain of the Cunard Line's *Carpathia*. Captain Arthur Rostron explained at the U.S. Senate Inquiry, in comparing the gross tonnage of his own ship as being 13,600 tons to *Titanic's* 46,328 tons, why they were both required to carry a total of 20 lifeboats each.

Carpathia was certified to carry 2,450 passengers, with a compliment of 300 crew members. Senator Smith asked Rostron "The fact that, under these regulations, you are obliged to carry 20 lifeboats and the *Titanic* was only obliged to carry 20, with her additional tonnage, indicates either that these regulations were prescribed long ago". Rostron replied "No, sir; it has nothing to do with that. What it has to do with is the ship itself. The ships are built nowadays to be practically unsinkable, and each ship is supposed to be a lifeboat in itself. The boats are merely supposed to be put on as a standby. The ships are supposed to be built, and the naval architects say they are, unsinkable under certain conditions. What the exact conditions are, I do not know, as to whether it is with alternate compartments full, or what it may be. That is why in our ship we carry more lifeboats, for the simple reason that we are built differently from the *Titanic*; differently constructed".

Under the 1883 Merchant Shipping Act, *Titanic* had more lifeboats than she was required to have. On her boat deck, the upper most deck. *Titanic* had 14 main lifeboats, 8 toward the aft and 6 toward the forward of the ship, 4 collapsible boats and 2 emergency cutters. The emergency cutters were held on their davits over the side of the ship in preparation for an emergency, such as a passenger falling over the side.

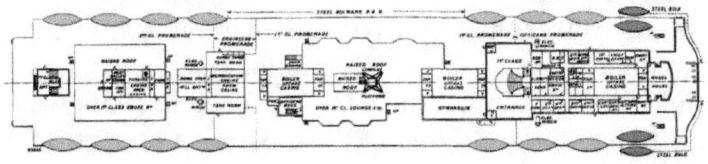

Titanic main lifeboats in light grey, Emergency cutter lifeboats in dark grey (outer), collapsible lifeboats - C and D – in dark grey. Two other collapsible lifeboats - A and B - are situated behind the crew quarters.

Titanic was woefully underprepared for the disaster that doomed her. Lifeboat drills had not been carried out since leaving Southampton. A lifeboat drill had been scheduled for the morning of the disaster, but for various reasons, had been cancelled by Captain Smith. Few members of crew were aware of their lifeboat stations or knew what they were supposed to do in the event of an emergency. A cursory drill had been carried out while the ship was docked at Southampton, including the launching of two boats, rowing them around the Wharf, then returning them to the ship.

White Star Line never envisaged that all the crew and passengers would have to evacuate the ship all at once, as *Titanic* was believed to be "practically unsinkable" and the lifeboats were intended to ferry passengers and crew from the stricken ship to rescue ships. This belief was reinforced for White Star Line during *Titanic's* construction, because their own *RMS Republic* was involved in a collision with the Lloyd Italiano liner, *SS Florida* in January 1909. Although *RMS Republic* sunk, her crew and passengers were all saved, because the ship stayed afloat long enough for them all to be ferried to rescue ships, who arrived to assist. *RMS Republic* stayed afloat considerably longer than *Titanic,* just under three hours as *RMS Republic* took half a day to sink. Another similar incident happened in 1956, when the Italian Liner *Andrea Doria* took eight hours to sink, which gave ample time for all passengers and crew to be ferried to safety.

~ ~ ~ ~

Boxhall alerted Captain Smith of a vessel forward of *Titanic's* position, about three miles off. A short discussion began between them that resulted in Boxhall firing off rockets and using a signal lamp to try to attract the ship's attention, without observing any response from the other vessel. At 12.25am, Smith gives the order to start loading the lifeboats, with women and children first.

The first lifeboat was launched from *Titanic* about 12.45am, 15 April, an hour after she struck the iceberg and 40 minutes after the first lifeboat was uncovered.

The boats were lowered in sequence, from the middle forward to aft. First Officer Murdoch, Third Officer Herbert Pitman and Fifth Officer Harold Lowe were working on the starboard side, with assistance from White Star Line Chairman, J Bruce Ismay and John Jacob Astor. Chief Officer Henry Wilde and 2nd Officer Charles Lightoller were working on the port side, while Captain Smith was on the bridge.

Smith's order of "Women and Children first" was interpreted differently between starboard and port. Lightoller interpreted the order as Women and Children only, where-as Murdoch interpreted it as Women and Children First on the boats, then if space allows, men are permitted to take the extra space. The result was, Lightoller launched many boats that were barely half full to capacity. Murdoch allowed men to evacuate in the boats if there were no further women and children nearby waiting to embark. Murdoch's actions significantly increased the number of men who survived the disaster.

Lifeboat 7, a standard lifeboat, was the first to be launched under the supervision of First Officer Murdoch, assisted by Ismay at 12.45am on the starboard side, with only 28 people onboard out of a capacity of 65 people.

One reason for this was, at this time, the passengers believed the activity to be merely an exercise, believing the ship to be in no immediate danger. Although Murdoch and Lowe had tried to persuade passengers to board, most were reluctant to do so.

Testimony from the later U.S senate inquiry into the *Titanic* disaster would claim the Officers believed the lifeboats were at risk of breaking apart if they were lowered at full to capacity. The Officers instead believed the boats would be further filled once they had reached the water from doors in the ships hull or would pick up people from the water. Although this did not happen when number 7 was launched, it did happen once the following boat was launched. An earlier test of the boats was carried out at Harland and Wolff, where the boats were lowered with full capacity. However, for some unknown reason, these test results were never passed on to *Titanic's* crew.

On the aft docking bridge - or Poop Deck - Quartermaster George Rowe continued on his rounds, totally oblivious to any happenings further forward, as he had seen nobody in over an hour. He watched in amazement as boat 7 drifted past on the starboard side. Rowe telephoned the main bridge to enquire if they were aware of a boat being lowered. A voice on the bridge enquired who he was. He replied, he was the stern lookout. It quickly became apparent he had been forgotten. Rowe was ordered to come forward and bring rockets with him. Rowe moved abruptly toward the bow, carrying a crate of 12 rockets under his arm.

The second boat launched was standard lifeboat number 5 from the starboard side, by Murdoch and Lowe, with assistance from Ismay and Third Officer Pitman at 12.53 am. The boat was loaded mainly with women and children. A few husbands were allowed to join their wives, after some of the crowd remarked "Put the brides and grooms in first." John Jacob Astor remarked "We are safer onboard the ship than in that little boat."

Still wearing pyjamas and slippers, Ismay urged Pitman to load Women and Children first. Pitman disagreed saying, "I await Captains orders." Smith was on the bridge and Pitman finally went to the Captain for approval. A short time later, Ismay urged a Stewardess to board. Pitman also boarded with Murdoch's approval and was placed in charge of boat 5.

Able-bodied seaman George Moore was put in charge of standard lifeboat 3 by Murdoch. Again, mainly women and children first, then followed by a few men before it was launched. A few times that night, men were helping their wives onto the boats, then standing back, accepting their fate of going down with the ship. Margaret Brown would later state during an interview with the *New York Times*: "The whole thing was so formal that it was difficult for anyone to realise it was a tragedy. Men and women stood in little groups and talked. Some laughed as the boats went over the side. All the time the band was playing ... I can see the men up on deck tucking in the women and smiling. It was a strange night. It all seemed like a play, like a dream that was being executed for entertainment. It did not seem real. Men would say 'After you' as they made some woman comfortable, then stepped back."

One notable example was First Class passenger Charles Melville Hays, a railroad manager of Montreal, Canada, who helped his wife onto lifeboat 3, then retreated and made no attempt to board any of the remaining lifeboats. Among the passengers on lifeboat 3 were the

Spedden family, of whom an earlier photo of Robert on deck playing with a spinning top was taken, who was only 6 years old at the time of the *Titanic* disaster. 40 year old, Governess Elizabeth Shutes, while describing the chaotic experience on boat 3, later wrote, "Our men knew nothing about the position of the stars, hardly how to pull together. Two oars were soon overboard. The men's hands were too cold to hold on. Then across the water swept that awful wail, the cry of those drowning people. In my ears I heard: 'She's gone, lads; row like hell or we'll get the devil of a swell."

The first lifeboat to depart from the port side was Boat 8, a standard lifeboat, at 1.00am, with Able-bodied seaman, Thomas Jones in charge. Second Officer, Lightoller was assisted by Chief Officer Wilde. Ida Strauss was asked to join the others in the boat, but she refused, saying, " I will not be separated from my husband - Isador Strauss. As we have lived, so we will die together". The 67 year old Isidor also refused an offer for them both saying " I do not wish any distinction in my favour which is not granted to others". Archibald Gracie witnessed what happened, saying "Then I saw Mr. Straus and Mrs. Straus, of whom I had seen a great deal, during the voyage. I had heard them discussing that if they were going to die, they would die together. We tried to persuade Mrs. Straus to go alone, without her husband, and she said no. Then we wanted to make an exception of the husband, too, because he was an elderly man, he said no, he would share his fate with the rest of the men, and that he would not go beyond. So I left them there." Both Isidor and Ida Strauss were last seen hand in hand, as the ship went down. Able-Bodied Seaman Jones praised the courage of 1st Class passenger, the Countess of Rothes, by stating: "I saw the way she was carrying herself and the quiet, determined manner in which she spoke, and I knew she was more of a man than most aboard, so I put her in command at the tiller. There was another woman in the boat who helped, and was every minute rowing. It was she who suggested we should sing, and we sang as we rowed, starting with *'Pull for the Shore.'* We were still singing when we saw the lights of the Carpathia, and then we stopped singing and prayed."

Titanic's fate is littered with stories of passengers refusing to leave the sinking ship on the available lifeboats, while others retiring back to their cabins and suites, facing their fate. History has seen these acts as bravery among many passengers. People tend to act on judgement, based on their knowledge. Many believed that Titanic was so large that no harm could come to them, if they just stayed calm and acted accordingly. There were no apparent signs of peril for the passengers and it must also be remembered, no evacuation or orders to abandon ship had been forthcoming from the Captain. Those passengers who refused to leave the safety of such a gigantic ship, were making judgment calls, based and acting on their knowledge.

The launch of emergency cutter lifeboat 1, was a departure from Murdoch's Women and Children First directive. After watching boat 3, being lowered into the cold Atlantic Ocean. Sir Cosmo Duff Gordon asked if his party could be loaded into boat 1.

Murdoch relented by also allowing a group of six Stokers and two American passengers, Abraham Soloman and C.E. Stengel, along with a Lookout George Symons, he had put in charge. Out of a capacity of 40, Murdoch was allowing boat 1 to launch with only twelve passengers aboard, which prompted Greaser, Walter Hurst to remark " If they are sending the boats away, they might as well put some people in them."

Among the passengers onboard boat 1, were the Duff-Gordons. The boat had a further capacity for another 28 people.

As was with most of the boats lowered from *Titanic* that night. There were no support from crew members to return to pick up additional survivors from the water.

Fireman Charles Hedrickson told them "its up to us to go back and pick up anyone in the water". He found no support. Lady Duff-Gordon exclaimed to her Secretary "Where has your beautiful night-dress gone". Fireman Pusey told the Duff-Gordons that the crew had lost all their kit and as from the moment *Titanic* sank, their pay will be stopped. To which Cosmo Duff-Gordon replied, " Very well, I will give you a fiver each to start a new kit!" Not realising the consequences of his actions, he did just that and proceeded to write a cheque for £5 for every crewman aboard.

Later he was accused of bribing the crew into not returning to the sunken liner to pick up additional survivors. From that moment on, his reputation sank along with the great *Titanic*. Later, after being rescued by the *Carpathia*, Sir Cosmo organised a group photo on *Carpathia's* foredeck of his party dressed in the life jackets, while the other survivors watched on, incredulously.

This photograph, looking up toward the bridge of Titanic, illustrates the starboard side emergency cutter lifeboat No 1, hanging over the side on its davit, in case of an emergency at sea.

Standard lifeboat 6 was launched at 1.10am, from the port side. From a capacity of 65 people, only 28 people occupied its seats. Quartermaster Robert Hitchens and lookout Frederick Fleet were placed in charge by Second Officer Lightoller. Among its occupants were Denver Millionairess and socialite Margaret Brown, who did not board voluntarily. She was picked up and thrown in bodily by a crewman.

Lightoller asked for additional rowers after protests from within the boat for additional rowers. Major Arthur Godfrey Peuchen of the Royal Canadian Yacht Club volunteered and shimmied down the falls to take a position as rower. The boat could only draw slowly away from *Titanic,* as Hitchens and Peuchin quarreled. Hitchens refused Peuchin's request to row. Margaret Brown was getting furious at their attitude and asked if the women could row to help keep warm. Hitchens refused that request.

An order came from the bridge from Captain Smith, to return the boat to pick up more passengers from the water. Hitchens refused to return saying "No, we are not going back to the ship. It's our lives now, not theirs". After *Titanic* had sunk, Margaret Brown, Peuchin and several others urged Hitchens to return to pick up survivors. Hitchens again refused, saying, "There's no use going back, 'cause there's only a lot of stiffs there". Brown threatened to throw him overboard, Hitchens protested, swore at her and told her to shut up! A stoker told him "Don't you know you are talking to a lady?" Brown then took charge of the tiller.

By 1.15 am, 7 lifeboats had been launched, with far fewer passengers and crew than they were rated for, although more people were beginning to fill them. The water was now up to *Titanic's* name-plate on her bow as she began to list to Port.

40 people were onboard standard lifeboat 16, launched from the port side aft at 1.20am. Sixth Officer James Moody supervised the loading of Stewardess, Violet Jessop - who had survived the collision of *RMS Olympic* with *HMS Hawke* the previous year and would go on to survive the sinking of *Britannic* in 1916, making her the only person to survive disasters on all three White Star Line's Olympic-Class Liners. Most of those, onboard lifeboat 16 were women and children from Second and Third Class.

When standard lifeboat 14 was launched at 1.25am from the port side aft, 58 people were onboard, as panic was beginning to become evident.

Titanic was well down in the water and passengers were beginning to press up against the rails. Lowe fired three shots from his revolver into the air to warn the crowd off. A young man jumped into the boat as it was being lowered into the Ocean. Lowe threatened to throw him overboard if he didn't get out of the boat, then appealed to him to "be a man - we've got women and children to save." The young man returned to the deck. Another male passenger managed to board boat 14 and conceal himself under a woman's shawl. Lowe took charge of the boat after the ship sank and it was Lowe who bundled boats 10, 12, 14 and collapsible D, before transferring many of those present on boat 14, then returned to the scene of the sinking to try to search and pick up survivors. That was the only rescue bid that night. Unfortunately, it came too late, because there were many hundreds of lifeless bodies floating, after dying from hypothermia. A few were picked up, but died soon after, although six of those picked up did survive. A few hours later, Lowe rescued the survivors on Collapsible A, which was in danger of sinking.

Panic was starting to sink in for those still onboard *Titanic*, as the seriousness of their situation was beginning to dawn on them. A male passenger jumped into standard lifeboat 12 from Deck B as it was being lowered from the port side aft at 1.30am. Lifeboat 12 was first put into the charge of Able-Bodied Seaman Frederick Clench, but was subsequently placed in charge of Able Seaman John Poigndestre.

Poingndestre had to use a knife to cut the ropes supporting the boat after difficulties occurred while unhooking the falls. After the sinking, several passengers were transferred from other boats, including boat 14, making boat 12 seriously overloaded with 69 people aboard.

Wireless distress calls from Philips were by then priority and had quickly reached desperation status. His messages had begun to contain phrases such as "we are sinking fast" and "we cannot last much longer."

Ismay and Moody continued assisting Murdoch with the launch of standard lifeboat number 9, from the starboard side aft of *Titanic* at 1.30am, with 56 passengers.

Boatswain's Mate, Albert Hames was put in charge with Able-Bodied Seaman George McGough manning the Tiller. Most of the passengers were women, with two or three men who entered when it was clear that no more women were present or didn't come forward.

May Futrelle, wife of Jacques Futrelle initially refused to leave her husband and board the boat, until he told her " For god's sake, go! It's your last chance! Go!" An Officer forced her into the boat. The millionaire Benjamin Guggenheim brought his mistress, Leontine Aubart, and her maid Emma Sagassar to boat 9, then quietly walked away back to his stateroom with his valet, Victor Giglio, where they both removed their lifejackets and put on their evening wear, before heading to the First Class Lounge. Guggenheim told a Steward "We're dressed in our best, and are prepared to go down like gentlemen. There is grave doubt that the men will get off. I am willing to remain and play the man's game, if there are not enough boats for more than the women and children. I won't die here like a beast. Tell my wife I played the game out straight and to the end.

When Ismay asked if there were any more women and children available, Kate Buss and her friend Marion Wright approached and noticed two shipboard acquaintances, Douglas Norman and Dr. Alfred Pain. Buss and Wright asked them to join them, but, the two men were barred from entering the boat by crewmen on the deck. Buss protested and demanded why they are not allowed to board. Haines told her "The officer gave the order to lower away, and if I didn't do so, he might shoot me, and simply put someone else in charge, and your friends would still not be allowed to come." They never saw Pain and Norman again.

By the time standard lifeboat number 11 was launched at 1.35am, under Murdoch's supervision, the boats were being filled more to capacity than previous boats - Boat 11, is believed to have had close to 70 people aboard. - Able-Bodied Seaman Sidney Humphreys was placed in charge. Steward James Witter had not intended to board the boat, but was knocked into it by a hysterical woman he was helping board as the boat was being lowered.

Illustration depicting the launching of Titanic's Lifeboats

A lucky toy pig, wrapped in a blanket, mistakenly believed to be a baby, was tossed in to one of the women aboard. The toy actually belonged to First Class passenger Edith Louise Rosenbaum, who could not bear to be parted with it.

Eight year old, Marshall Drew was also in boat 11, with his Aunt and Uncle. He later said about his experience in boat 11:"When the *Titanic* struck the iceberg, I was in bed. However, for whatever reason I was awake and remember the jolt and cessation of motion. A steward knocked on the stateroom door and directed us to get dressed, put on life preservers and go to the boat deck, which we did. The steward as we passed was trying to arouse passengers who had locked themselves in for the night. Elevators were not running. We walked up to the boat deck. All was calm and orderly. An officer was in charge. 'Women and children first,' he said, as he directed lifeboat number 11 to be filled."

"There were many tearful farewells. We and Uncle Jim said good-bye. The lowering of the lifeboat, 70 feet to the sea was perilous. Davits, ropes, nothing worked properly, so that first one end of the lifeboat was tilted up and then far down. I think it was the only time I was scared. Lifeboats pulled some distance away from the sinking *Titanic*, afraid of what suction might do. As row by row of the porthole lights of the *Titanic* sank into the sea this was about all one could see. When the *Titanic* upended to sink, all was blacked out until the tons of machinery crashed to the bow. As this happened hundreds and hundreds of people were thrown into the sea."

"It isn't likely I shall ever forget the screams of these people, as they perished in water said to be 28 degrees. At this point in my life I was being brought up as a typical British kid. You were not allowed to cry. You were a 'little man.' So as a cool kid I lay down in the bottom of the lifeboat and went to sleep. When I awoke it was broad daylight as we approached the *Carpathia*. Looking around over the gunwale it seemed to me like the Arctic. Icebergs of huge size ringed the horizon for 360 degrees."

Wireless operator Jack Philips sent the last "intelligible" message to the Russian steamer, *Birma* at about 1.40am, saying "SOS SOS CQD cqd - MGY We are sinking fast, passengers being put into lifeboats". MGY.

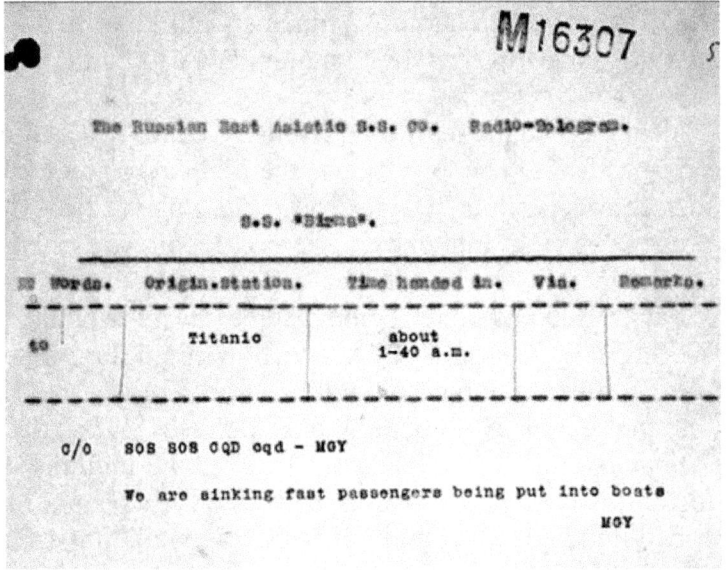

Distress message to SS Birma from Jack Philips at about 1.40am, 15 April 1912

The Boat deck and A Deck is where Standard Lifeboat 13 was loaded from before it was launched at 1.40am from the starboard side, under the supervision of Murdoch, Moody and Ismay, heavily loaded with 65 people, mainly Second and Third Class women and children and a few men, including Lawrence Beesley who subsequently wrote a popular book about the *Titanic* disaster and Dr. Washington Dodge, who was persuaded by Steward F. Dent Ray to take his family on the maiden voyage of *Titanic*, after seeing his family embark on Boat 5.

Eleven Year old, Ruth Becker had bought blankets from her state room onto boat 13. These were later used to keep the stokers warm who were rowing in sleeveless shirts in the freezing air above decks. While the boat was being lowered, problems became apparent as a stream of water was being expelled through the ship's condenser exhausts, in a vain attempt to curb and expel the water that was rapidly flooding *Titanic*. The occupants of the boat had to use oars and spars to guide the boat past the four foot wide stream.

Boat 13, was being lowered simultaneously with boat 15 and came close to crushing the occupants of boat 13, as boat 15 was lowered on top of it. The lowering of boat 15 was halted just in time to prevent further injury on boat 13. The ropes or falls supporting boat 13 became jammed and had to be cut free to allow the boat to pull away from the side of *Titanic*.

Fireman Frank Dyamond was placed in charge of the most heavily laden boat at launching, standard lifeboat 15, from the starboard side with 65 people onboard. Murdoch and Moody oversaw the loading of the boat that, when launched, caused the gunwale to be well down in the water. Boat 15 was launched simultaneously as boat 13 and reached the water only a minute later at 1.41am.

Lifeboat 2, from the port side was the second emergency cutter, which was normally hung on its davit over the side, in case of a passenger falling over the side of the ship, or any other emergency at sea where a boat has to be launched at short notice.

The cutters were each capable of carrying up the 40 people, as opposed to the standard lifeboats, with a capacity of 65 people each.

Fourth Officer Boxhall was placed in command of boat 2 with 25 people onboard. Lightoller moved to load boat 2, but found it already half full of men. He ordered them all out at gun point, saying "Get out of there, you damned cowards! I'd like to see every one of you overboard!" The men involved had no way of knowing that Lightoller's revolver was not loaded.

They removed themselves from the boat. As a result, lifeboat 2 was lowered with 17 people onboard, with 16 mostly Third Class women and one male Third Class passenger.

After *Titanic* had sunk, Boxhall suggested he take the boat back to pick up any survivors but the passengers hotly refused. Boxhall found that rather puzzling because it was only a short time before that the women were urging Lightoller to allow their husbands on with them. Now, they did not want to go back to save them.

Standard lifeboat 10 was launched at 1.50am. Able-bodied Seaman, Edward Buley, was placed in charge by Murdoch, with 35 people aboard, about half its capacity.

At this time *Titanic* was listing to port, making it increasingly difficult to launch the lifeboats from the port side as the list had created a growing gap of about 3 feet - 0.9 m - from the port side of the ship to the side of the boats. A French woman who tried to board the boat fell between the ship and the boat but was saved from falling and managed to board the boat. *Titanic's* list created an urgency to load the lifeboats, children were rushed aboard. One baby was tossed in and was caught by a woman passenger. Mary Graham Carmichael Marvin, who was on her honeymoon on *Titanic* later commented "As I was put into the boat, he cried to me, 'It's all right, little girl. You go. I will stay.' As our boat shoved off, he threw me a kiss, and that was the last I saw of him."

The last standard lifeboat to launch from *Titanic*, was Boat 4 from the port side, under the supervision of Second Officer Lightoller. Boat 4 was launched simultaneously with boat 10, from the starboard side at 1.50am.

Captain Smith said the last two boats should be loaded from the Promenade Deck, instead of the Boat Deck, because the ship's angle in the water was increasing. Smith seems to have been confusing *Titanic* and her sister ship *Olympic* at this stage, seeming to forget, the forward part of the Promenade Deck on *Titanic* was enclosed. As opposed to *Olympic's*, which was open.

Lightoller ordered the glass enclosures to be opened, but was faced immediately with difficulties. First, the windows were unexpectedly difficult to open and the boat got tangled up on the ships Sounding Spar, which projected from the hull immediately below the cutter. The spar had to be chopped off to allow the lifeboat to be launched.

Boarding also presented difficulties. To overcome this, deck-chairs were placed between the windows and the boat to allow passengers to transfer safely. The pregnant, Madeleine Astor was assisted aboard the boat by her husband, John Jacob Astor, who asked Lightoller if he could join her. Lightoller refused his request, saying "No men are allowed in these boats until the women are loaded first". Astor told his wife "The Sea is calm. You're in good hands. I'll meet you in the morning." He did not survive.

Quartermaster Walter Perkis was placed in charge of boat 4, which when launched had 40 women and 2 crew members aboard. Perkis instructed the boat be rowed around the sinking ship, to pick up passengers from the open gangways. At one point, he found himself below the empty Davit of boat No 16, where two greasers, Thomas Ranger and Frederick William Scott, shimmied down the falls toward boat 4. Scott fell into the water but was hauled onboard. To avoid the effects of the suction, Perkis ordered the boat away from *Titanic*. A lamp trimmer, Samuel Ernest Hemming jumped from *Titanic* and swam the 200 yards to boat 4. Immediately after the sinking, Perkis ordered the boat back to pick up survivors. He picked up another eight from the freezing north Atlantic: Fireman Thomas Patrick Dillon, Seaman William Henry Lyons, Stewards Andrew Cunningham and Sidney Conrad Siebert, Storekeeper Frank Winnold Prentice and two unidentified survivors. Later, the numbers increased after some were transferred from boat14 and Collapsible Boat D. Making a total of 60 occupants.

Nearer My God To Thee

Just as *Titanic* has famously remained in the imagination of the modern world, so has the tune the string band is believed to have played as the ship sank, *"Nearer My God To Thee"*. The lyrics were written by, the English poet Sarah Fuller Flower Adams in 1841.

The lyrics were put to music in 1861, to the tune '*Horbury*' and later to the tune of '*Bethany*', written in 1859.

Titanic survivor, Stewardess and Nurse, Violet Jessop in her account of the disaster claimed in 1934, she heard the tune played as *Titanic* sank beneath the surface. In another account, survivor Archibald Gracie IV in his book *The Truth About The Titanic*, published in 1913, emphatically denies the tune was played by the ship's ensemble. Wireless operator, Harold Bride in an interview with a *New York Times* journalist, after *Carpathia* reached New York also confirms *Nearer My God To Thee* was not played as *Titanic* began its descent to the cold dark sea bed of the North Atlantic.

Bride claims the popular waltz *Autumn*, or the Episcopalian hymn *Songe d'Automne or Autumn Dream*, was played by Wallace Hartley and the string ensemble. Part of Bride's comments to the journalist included:

"I saw a collapsible boat near a funnel and went towards it. I looked out. The boat deck was awash."
"From aft came the tunes of the band. It was a rag-time tune, I don't know what. Then there was '*Autumn*'. Phillips ran aft, and that was the last time I saw him alive."

"I went to the place I had seen the collapsible boat on the boat deck, and to my surprise I saw the boat and the men still trying to push it off. I guess there wasn't a sailor in the crowd. They couldn't do it. I went up to them and was just lending a hand when a large wave came awash of the deck. The big wave carried the boat off with it."

"Smoke and sparks were rushing out of the funnel. There must have been an explosion, but we had heard none. We only saw the big stream of sparks. The ship was gradually turning on its nose - just like a duck does that goes down for a dive. I had only one thing on my mind - to get away from the suction. The band was still playing. I guess all of the band went down."

"They were playing "*Autumn*" then. I swam with all my might. I suppose I was 150 feet away when the *Titanic*, up on her nose and with her after quarter sticking up in the air, began to settle - slowly."

"The way the band kept playing was a noble thing. I heard it first while still we were working the wireless, then there was a rag-time tune for us, and the last I saw of the band, when I was floating out in the sea with my lifebelt on, it was still on deck playing "*Autumn*". How they ever did it I cannot imagine."

Titanic Band: Top left - Theodore Brailey - pianist, Top right - Roger Bricoux – Cellist

Middle left - Percy C. Taylor - Cellist, Centre - Wallace Hartley - Bandmaster, violist, Middle right - George Krins - violist.

Bottom left - John Hume - First violinist, Bottom right - J. Fred C. Clark - Bass violist.

Missing from picture - J. W. Woodward - Cellist

Bride's account carries some weight, as being a wireless operator, he had to rely largely on detail. His account to the *New York Times* journalist indicates he was not excited or anxious during the final moments of *Titanic*. He was rather cool headed and able to recollect in his mind with reasonable accuracy, as opposed to another who may be panicky and anxious for their own life in such a situation. Or the confusion and grief of saying goodbye and worrying if loved ones are going to survive to reunite, while fully in the knowledge that a large number of fellow travelers would not survive and would be lost with *Titanic*.

Many other survivors apart from Jessop, Gracie and Bride recollected the final tune played by the ships band. The majority of them all have the same consensus that *"Nearer My God To Thee"* was indeed the final tune played.

There are two popular versions of the Christian hymn, one being the American version *Bethany* and the English version *Horbury*. Both tunes are distinctly different from each other, neither sounds the remotest similar. In short, it would be impossible to confuse the two versions. But accounts from the *Titanic* disaster, from the survivors, both American and British, claim, both versions were played by Hartley and the other members of the band.

Band leader, Wallace Hartley was born in Colne, Lancashire, England in 1878. His father, a Methodist choirmaster introduced Wallace to the *Horbury* version of the hymn, where it was played regularly at their Methodist Sunday services and where Wallace learned to play the violin from a fellow congregation member.

Many publications and movies about *Titanic* insist on portraying *"Nearer My God To Thee"* as the last tune Wallace Hartley and the other seven members played as the ship foundered. Walter Lords book, *"A Night To Remember"* presents Harold Bride's account. That of *"Autumn" - Songe d'Automne.* The 1958 movie by Roy Ward Baker of the same name features the *Bethany* version of the hymn, as does James Cameron's 1997 movie *"Titanic".* On the other hand, Jean Negulesco's 1953 movie *"Titanic"* features the *Horbury* version of the hymn. Hundreds of other books written since 1912, all mention *"Nearer My God To Thee"* without mentioning either particular tune version.

The origins of the last tune played on *Titanic*, being *"Nearer My God To Thee"* could be founded on the grounding and destruction of Red Star Lines, *SS Valencia* on the South Shore of Vancouver Island on September 23, 1906.

As the lifeboats were being loaded and launched on *Valencia*, The passengers and crew began singing, *"Nearer My God To Thee"*. The memory of *SS Valencia* could have remained among the passengers of *Titanic*, among tunes they heard from the band of *Titanic*.

Another twist of the question of the bands final tune is, a third version. That written by Sir Arthur Sullivan from Gilbert and Sullivan fame. called *"Propior Doe"*. Hartley was a good friend of Sir Arthur Sullivan. *"Propior Doe, Nearer My God To Thee"* was a personal favourite of Hartley.

In the British national tabloid newspaper, *The Daily Sketch*, on April 22, 1912. A one time colleague of Hartley's said that, when working on the Cunard Lines, *Mauretania*. Hartley had commented that, in the event of being on the deck of a sinking ship, He would like to play, *"O God Our Help In Ages Past."*

However, *"Nearer My God To Thee"* has gained popular acceptance.

~ ~ ~ ~

The first of the Collapsible Engelhardt lifeboats to be launched was Collapsible boat C, which was retrieved from its stored position and attached to the davits. It was supervised by Murdoch and assisted by Ismay and Moody.

By this time, *Titanic's* bow was dipping deep into the water. The majority of the remaining passengers were moving aft toward the stern. Purser McElroy discharged two shots into the air from his revolver to discourage a large group of Stewards and Third Class passengers from storming the boat.

While Murdoch tried to hold the crowd back, Hugh Woolner and Swedish Army Lieutenant Bjorn Steffanson came to Murdoch's assistance, by dragging two Stewards out, who had made it into the boat. As the deck was relatively clear of passengers, Ismay assisted those present into the boat, then, walked a distance, calling out for more women to load before launching Collapsible C, but he could not find any.

Quartermaster George Rowe was placed in charge of Collapsible C. Murdoch, Wilde and Ismay repeatedly asked if there were more women to come forward. A number of men took the remaining seats, including J Bruce Ismay and William Carter. As the boat was being lowered, the boat scraped down the hull of *Titanic*, as the port side list was increasing dramatically. At 2.00am, Collapsible C was the last boat launched from the Starboard side.

Two illustrations depicting the sad partings and hopelessness onboard Titanic.

By 2,00 am *Titanic* was well down in the water. The cold North Atlantic was only about ten feet below the Promenade Deck, 1.500 people remained on *Titanic* by the time Collapsible D was being prepared for launching. Band Leader Wallace Hartley was now choosing the last tune his band would play. Some survivors claim the final tune was *"Nearer My God To Thee."*

Crew members had to form a cordon around Collapsible D to prevent a storm of passengers boarding. Women and children were still picked out for placements. A male passenger, Louis Hoffman came forward with two boys. His name was later identified as Michel Navratil, who was a Slovak tailor.

After kidnapping his two boys from his estranged wife, he took them onboard *Titanic* to make a new life in the United States. The two boys, gained the popular name of the '*Titanic Orphans*" as their father did not survive the disaster. The boys were later identified as Michel Marcel and Edmond Navratil after their mother identified them from photos that were published of them, around the world.

Quartermaster Arthur Bright was placed in charge with 25 people onboard, as the boat was lowered from *Titanic's* port side. Two First Class passengers, Hugh Woolner and Mauritz Haken Bjornstrom-Steffanson jumped into the boat, as it was being lowered from A Deck, even as A. Deck itself was continuing to flood.

Bjornstrom-Steffanson landed upside down in the boat's bow, Woolner landed half-way out, before being pulled aboard. Another First Class passenger, Frederick Maxfield jumped into the water after assisting his wife in the boat and was plucked out by the occupants.

Titanic's tilt grows deeper by 2.05 am as water poured onto the forward section of A. Deck. At this time, Captain Smith was beginning his final inspection. Smith went to the wireless room and relieved Philips and Bride, and told them "Your duty is done."

On his way back to the bridge, Smith told several crewmen "Its every man for himself now."

Collapsible A and B proved difficult to retrieve and prepare from their respective storage areas from atop the Officers quarters. Lightoller, Murdoch, Moody and Bride had to rig makeshift ramps from oars and spars to lower them onto the Boat deck as *Titanic's* bow section continued to sink up to and over the bridge.

Unfortunately, the makeshift ramp collapsed under collapsible Boat B, resulting in the Boat landing up-side down on the Deck. There was no time to right it as *Titanic* had begun her breakup and plunge to the bottom of the Atlantic Ocean. A rapid movement of the ship caused a massive wave to ride along the Boat deck, washing the boat away from the stricken liner and washing many people over the side. Wireless operator Harold Bride was washed from the deck, the turbulent water from the wash, dragging him under. When he surfaced again he found himself trapped under the overturned hull.

The stays supporting the forward funnel snapped under the strain. Crashing into the water, the toppling funnel crushed swimmers beneath it, creating a wave that pushed the boat away from the sinking vessel. As the ship sank, the lifeboat was left amongst hundreds of people in the water. Several dozen, including Lightoller managed to climb onboard and take charge. Bride managed to escape out of the upturned hull and climb aboard. Archibald Gracie and Jack Thayer, also managed to climb aboard. In its present state, the boat was not stable, throughout the next few hours, the air under the boat escaped, lowering it further into the water, exposing those onboard to the water, first their feet, then their ankles, followed by their knees. Many of those who managed to climb aboard perished as the freezing temperature of the air and water exhausted them. Towards the Dawn, the water became choppy.

Lightoller organised the remaining men on the hull to stand up in two parallel lines, either side of the centre keel, facing the bow. Then got them to sway in unison to counteract the rocking motion, created by the swell. Out of the original dozens, only 14 were left alive when they were finally rescued.

Murdoch and Moody managed to get Collapsible Lifeboat A on deck the right way up, before the same wave that ejected Collapsible B from *Titanic*, also washed Collapsible A into the water at 2.12am. As a result, the boat floated away from *Titanic* without its canvas sides pulled up. It was dangerously low in the water and overloaded. Most of its occupants had climbed in from the water and died of hypothermia. After the ordeal, 13 people were left alive from Collapsible A.

CHAPTER EIGHT

Date With Destiny

"I knew Captain Smith for over fifteen years. Our conversation that night amounted to little or nothing. I simply sympathized with him on the accident; but at that time, as I then never expected to be saved, I did not want to bother him with questions, as I knew he had all he wanted to think of. He did suggest that I go down to A deck and see if there was not a boat alongside. This I did, and to my surprise saw the boat "D" still hanging on the davits and it occurred to me that if I swam out and waited for her to shove off they would pick me up, which was what happened."

- First-Class passenger, Frederick Hoyt.

Captain Smith carried out his final inspection of the Boat Deck at the time the final lifeboat - Collapsible D - was being lowered, telling the wireless operators and other crew members, they had done a great job, then later, upon his return to the Bridge - "Now its every man for himself."

Father Thomas Byles was giving absolutions and taking confessions, as the remaining passengers and crew were headed for the stern, shuffling past *Titanic's* band as they continued to play outside the ships gymnasium. Among them Archibald Gracie, who found his way blocked by "A mass of humanity" several lines deep as hundreds of Third Class passengers had made their way to the boat deck. Gracie gave up on the idea of going aft and jumped into the water to escape the crowd before him. Gracie later provided a chilling testimony.

Saying, "Soon after that - he had helped lower a lifeboat - the water came up on the boat deck. We saw it and heard it...Mr. Smith [his friend Clint Smith] and myself thought then that there was no more chance for us there, there were so many people at that particular point, so we decided to go toward the stern, still on the starboard side, and as we were going toward the stern, to our surprise and consternation, up came from the decks below a mass of humanity, men and women - and we had thought that all the women were already loaded into the boats. The water was then right by us, and we tried to jump, Mr. Smith and myself did."

Others were obviously making no attempt to escape. The ships designer, Thomas Andrews was last seen in the First Class smoking room, without a lifejacket and staring at the painting above the fireplace. The fate of Captain Smith remains unknown. The popular folklore dictates that he entered the ships bridge, closed the door into the wheelhouse, then held the ships wheel until the windows between the bridge and the wheelhouse exploded under the pressure of the water, that had flooded the bridge, then drowned "at the wheel."

Several passengers stated differently. Some claim he entered the bridge, then shot himself. Others claim he did indeed commit suicide. Marconi operator Bride claims he saw him jump into the water from the bridge.

At about 02:15 am, water was pouring into previously unflooded parts of the ship, through deck hatches, causing *Titanic's* angle in the water to increase rapidly. This rapid angle increase caused a giant wave to wash along the ship from the forward end of the boat deck - according to survivor Archibald Gracie IV - washing many people into the sea as collapsible lifeboats A and B were being cut from their lashings above the crew quarters by Gracie, Chief Officer Henry Wilde, First Officer Murdoch and Second Officer Charles Lightoller. Gracie, Bride and Lightoller were able to get onto the upturned hull of Collapsible B. But, Murdoch and Wilde perished in the water.

Second Officer Lightoller later recollected:

"Just then the ship took a slight but definite plunge - probably a bulkhead went - and the sea came rolling along up in a wave, over the steel fronted bridge, along the deck below us, washing the people back in a dreadful huddled mass. Those that didn't disappear under the water right away, instinctively started to clamber up that part of the deck still out of water, and work their way towards the stern, which was rising steadily out of the water as the bow went down. It was a sight that doesn't bear dwelling on - to stand there, above the wheelhouse, and on our quarters, watching the frantic struggles to climb up the sloping deck, utterly unable to even hold out a helping hand."

Lightoller decided to abandon the ship to escape the growing crowd and jumped into the sea from near the bridge. The water, rushing into a ventilation shaft, sucked Lightoller in until a massive blast of hot air blew him clear, he emerged next to the upturned lifeboat B. The forward funnel collapsed under its own weight, narrowly missing the boat, while crushing several people in the water. The surge from the wave washed the boat 50 yards or 46 metres from the sinking ship.

Lightoller would describe that moment: "When - floating in the dark - "I recognised my surroundings, we were full fifty yards clear of the ship. Lights on board the *Titanic* were still burning, and a wonderful spectacle she made, standing out black and massive against the starlit sky. Myriads of lights still gleaming through the portholes from that part of the decks, still above water."

At this time, *Titanic* was suffering immense stresses throughout her structure. First class passenger Jack Thayer described it:

"Occasionally there had been a muffled thud or deadened explosion within the ship. Now, without warning she seemed to start forward, moving forward and into the water at an angle of about fifteen degrees. This movement with the water rushing up toward us was accompanied by a rumbling roar, mixed with more muffled explosions. It was like standing under a steel railway bridge while an express train passes overhead mingled with the noise of a pressed steel factory and wholesale breakage of china."

Lawrence Beesley and other eyewitnesses say they saw *Titanic's* stern lifting high into the air at an angle of 30-45 degrees. As Beesley put it, "revolving apparently around a centre of gravity just astern of amidships". Other survivors described a great noise as attributed to Boiler explosions. Lawrence Beesley, in lifeboat 13 described the loud noise as: "partly a groan, partly a rattle, and partly a smash, and it was not a sudden roar as an explosion would be: it went on successively for some seconds, possibly fifteen to twenty". He attributed it to "the engines and machinery coming loose from their bolts and bearings, and falling through the compartments, smashing everything in their way."

About a minute later, the lights on *Titanic* went out, plunging the great ship into darkness. Jack Thayer recalled " groups of the fifteen hundred people still aboard, clinging in clusters or benches, like swarming bees; only to fall in masses, pairs or singly as the great after part of the ship, rose into the sky."

From upturned collapsible lifeboat B, Lightoller recollected "The fore part, and up to the second funnel was by this time completely submerged, and as we watched this terribly awe-inspiring sight, suddenly all the lights went out and the huge bulk was left in black darkness, but clearly silhouetted against the bright sky."

The weight of the water dragging the ship forward of the bridge into the water, combined with the air still inside the stern section, meant there were great opposing forces - which were concentrated on one weak area of the ships structure, the area of the engine room hatch. The ship split apart.

The Breakup

Two main theories existed for decades after the *Titanic* disaster. One school of thought suggested the vessel split in half. Another suggested the ship, in its final stages, did not split but instead went to the bottom of the Atlantic intact.

Seventeen year old, Jack Thayer who had jumped from the starboard side of the ship, near the second funnel just moments before the ship split said:

"The cold was terrific. The shock of the water took the breath out of my lungs. Down and down I went, spinning in all directions. Swimming as hard as I could in the direction, which I thought to be away from the ship, I finally came up with my lungs bursting, but not having taken any water. The ship was in front of me, forty yards away. How long I had been swimming under water, I don't know. Perhaps a minute or less."

"The water was over the base of the first funnel. The mass of people on board were surging back, always back towards the floating stern. Suddenly the whole superstructure of the ship appeared to split, well forward to mid-ship, and bow or buckle upwards. The second funnel, large enough for two automobiles to pass through abreast, seemed to be lifted off, emitting a cloud of sparks. It looked as if it would fall on top of me. It missed me by twenty or thirty feet. The suction of it drew me down and down, struggling and swimming, practically spent."

"As I finally came to the surface I put my hand over my head, in order to push away any obstruction. My hand came against something smooth and firm with rounded shape. I looked up, and realized that it was the cork fender of one of the collapsible lifeboats, which was floating in the water bottom side up. About four or five men were clinging to her bottom. I pulled myself up as far as I could, almost exhausted, but could not get my legs up. I asked them to give me a hand up, which they readily did. Sitting on my haunches and holding on for dear life, I was again facing the *Titanic.*"

"There was the gigantic mass, about fifty or sixty yards away. The forward motion had stopped. She was pivoting on a point just abaft of mid-ship. Her stern was gradually rising into the air, seemingly in no hurry, just slowly and deliberately. We could see groups of the almost fifteen hundred people still aboard, clinging in clusters or bunches, like swarming bees; only to fall in masses, pairs or singly, as the great after part of the ship, two hundred and fifty feet of it, rose into the sky, till it reached a sixty-five or seventy degree angle. Here it seemed to pause, and just hang, for what felt like minutes. Gradually she turned her deck away from us, as though to hide from our sight the awful spectacle. Then, with the deadened noise of the bursting of her last few gallant bulkheads, she slid quietly away from us into the sea."

Thayer had witnessed the ship splitting in two, shortly after jumping into the water because he was very close to the remaining stern section. The gigantic mass he mentioned would be the interior of the stern section, after its break from the forward section, which settled back on the surface before it was raised again. However, not all surviving passengers saw the ship break before the stern rose again into the sky.

A Second-class passenger from lifeboat No. 13 said:

"We could see her now only as the stern and some 150 feet of her stood outlined against the star-specked sky, looming black in the darkness, and in this position she continued for some minutes - I think as much as five minutes, but it may have been less. Then, first sinking back a little at the stern, I thought, she slid slowly forwards through the water and dived slantingly down; the sea closed over her and we had seen the last of the beautiful ship on which we had embarked four days before at Southampton."

The 1985 expedition that discovered the wreck of the *Titanic*, led by Dr Robert Ballard, confirmed the ship did indeed break in two during its sinking and plunge to the bottom of the Atlantic ocean in 1912.

~ ~ ~ ~

The split would have caused the forward part of the stern to flood very rapidly. Making the stern rise to its tilt of a vertical position of 90 degrees, where it remained for a few moments. Jack Thayer reported that the stern turned slightly on the surface, "gradually turning her deck away from us. Then with the deadened noise of the bursting of her last few gallant bulkheads, she slid quietly away from us into the sea."

Quartermaster Robert Hitchens later recounted his experience to Journalist Carlos F. Hurd, onboard the *Carpathia*. He was intending to present his evidence at any subsequent marine inquiry into the sinking of *Titanic*. Hitchens told Hurd:

"I went on watch at eight O'clock Sunday night and stood by the man at the wheel until ten. At ten I took the wheel for two hours."

"On the bridge from ten o'clock were First Officer Murdoch, Fourth Officer Boxhall and Sixth Officer Moody. In the crow's nest were Fleet and another man whose name I don't know."

"Second Officer Lightoller, who was on watch while I stood by, carrying messages and the like, from eight to ten, sent me soon after eight to tell the carpenter to look out for the fresh water supply, as it might be in danger of freezing. The temperature was then 31 degrees, he gave the crows nest a strict order to look out for small icebergs."

"Second Officer Lightoller was relieved by First Officer Murdoch at ten, and I took the wheel then. At 11.40 three gongs sounded from the crows nest, the signal for ' something right ahead'. At the same time one of the men in the crows-nest telephoned to the bridge that there was a large iceberg right ahead. As officer Murdoch's hand was on the lever to stop the engines the crash came. He stopped the engines, then immediately by another lever, closed the water-tight doors."

"The skipper - Captain Smith - came from the chart-room on to the bridge. His first words were 'Close the emergency doors'. Murdoch replied, 'They are already closed sir.'"

"Send to the carpenter and tell him to sound the ship', was the skippers next order. The carpenter never came up to report. He was probably the first man on that ship to lose his life."

"The skipper looked at the commutator, which shows in what direction the ship is listing. He saw that she carried five degrees list to the starboard."

"The ship was then rapidly settling forward. All the steam sirens were blowing. By the skipper's orders, given in the next few minutes, the engines were put to work at pumping out the ship, distress signals were sent by Marconi and rockets were sent up from the bridge by Quartermaster Rowe. All hands were ordered on deck and life belts were issued to the crew and every passenger."

"The Stewards and other hands helped the sailors in getting the boats out. The order 'women and children first' was given and enforced. There was no panic."

"I was at the wheel until 12.25. It was my duty to stay there until relieved. I was not relieved by anyone else, but was simply sent away by Second Officer Lightoller, who told me to take charge of a certain boat and load it with ladies."

"I did so, and there were thirty-two ladies, a sailor and myself in the boat when it was lowered, some time after 1 o'clock - I can't be sure of the time."

"The *Titanic* had sixteen lifeboats and two collapsible boats. All of them got away loaded, except that one of the collapsibles did not open properly and was used as a raft. Forty sailors and stewards who were floating in the water, got on this raft, and later had to abandon the raft., and were picked up by the different boats. Some others were floating about on chairs when picked up."

"Every boat, so far as I saw, was full when it was lowered, and every boat that set out reached the Carpathia. The green light on one of the boats helped to keep us together, but there were other lights. One was an electric flashlight that a gentleman had carried in his pocket."

"Our boat was 400 yards away when the ship went down. The suction nearby must have been terrific, but we were only rocked somewhat."

"I have told only what I know, and what I shall tell any marine court that may examine me."

Second Officer Lightoller, still clinging to the upturned hull of collapsible lifeboat B said "This unparalleled tragedy, that was being enacted before our very eyes, now rapidly approached its finale, as the huge ship slowly but surely reared herself on end and brought rudder and propellers clear of the water, till, at last, she assumed an absolute perpendicular position. In this amazing attitude she remained for the space of half a minute. Then with impressive majesty and ever-increasing momentum, she silently took her last tragic dive to seek a final resting place in the unfathomable depths of the cold gray Atlantic."

At 2.20am on Monday, April 15 1912, four days into her maiden voyage from Southampton to New York, *Titanic* sank at Latitude 41.46 N, Longitude 50.14 W. North Atlantic Ocean.

First Class passenger, Archibald Gracie jumped from the stern of the ship as she went under the surface. He described the event; "After sinking with the ship, it appeared to me as if I was propelled by some great force through the water. This might have been occasioned by explosions under the water, and I remembered fearful stories of people being boiled to death. Again and again I prayed for deliverance, although I felt sure that the end had come. I had the greatest difficulty in holding my breath until I came to the surface. I knew that once I inhaled, the water would suffocate me. When I got under water I struck out with all my strength for the surface. I got to air again after a time, which seemed to me to be unending. There was nothing in sight save the ocean, dotted with ice and strewn with large masses of wreckage. Dying men and women all about me were groaning and crying piteously. By moving from one piece of wreckage to another, at last I reached a cork raft. Soon the raft became so full that it seemed as if she would sink if more came on board her. The crew for self-preservation had therefore to refuse to permit any others to climb aboard. This was the most pathetic and horrible scene of all. The piteous cries of those around us still ring in my ears, and I will remember them to my dying day. 'hold on to what you have, old boy!' we shouted to each man who tried to get on board. 'One more of you would sink us all!' Many of those whom we refused answered as they went to their death, 'Good luck – God bless you!'"

As the pride of White Star Line was enveloped by the freezing, dark North Atlantic Ocean, the air was overcome with complete silence for a few moments. Then came the yells and agonising cries from the many who were left floating in the icy cold waters.

"There arose to the sky the most horrible sounds ever heard by mortal man except by those of us who survived this terrible tragedy. The agonising cries of death from over a thousand throats, the wails and groans of the suffering - none of us will ever forget to our dying day." - Colonel Archibald Gracie IV.

J. Bruce Ismay

Joseph Bruce Ismay was born in Crosby, Lancashire, a small town near Liverpool, England on 12 December, 1862. The son of Thomas Henry Ismay, and Margaret. J. Bruce Ismay became Chairman and managing director of White Star Line after the death of his father in 1899. White Star Line flourished under his control.

In 1901, the White Star Line was merged into an American conglomerate, the International Mercantile Marine Company, which incorporated several American and British shipping lines for the lucrative Atlantic shipping routes. Ismay became President of the IMM.

Before his father's death, Ismay was an American based agent for White Star Line in New York. While there, he met with the American News Paper tycoon, William Randolph Hearst. On several occasions, Ismay refused to cooperate with Hearst and the press, which led to a falling out between Ismay and Hearst.

William Randolph Hearst was a dubious businessman who had built the largest chain of newspapers throughout the United States of America, including the *San Francisco Examiner* and the *New York Journal*. He became well known for his style of journalism, being described as Sensationalist. A book was published in 1990 called *Unreliable Sources*, in which the two authors, Martin Lee and Norman Soloman, described Hearst's journalism approach as Yellow Journalism, noting that Hearst routinely invented sensational stories, faked interviews, ran phoney pictures and distorted real events. William Randolph Hearst's approach to journalism is commonly referred to in the 21st century as 'Gutter Journalism.'

At the time, Ismay had no idea how this fallout with Hearst would adversely affect his future and how a mogul like Hearst, with syndicated newspapers throughout the United States, would use his considerable power and influence, not only to spread lies and rumours about the events of 14 April 1912, but also would destroy the rest of Ismay's life, by means of a syndicated smear campaign.

After his father's death, Ismay pursued the building of four new ocean liners for the White Star Line fleet - dubbed 'The Big Four': *RMS Celtic, RMS Cedric, RMS Baltic* and *RMS Adriatic*. 'The Big Four' were designed more for luxury and speed than safety.

In 1907, Ismay wanted to add three more larger, more luxurious ships to his White Star fleet, dubbing them Olympic-class ocean liners. *RMS Olympic, RMS Titanic* and *RMS Britannic*. To this end, Ismay met with Lord Pirrie of the Harland and Wolff shipyards, in London, to discuss White Star Lines answer to Cunard's *RMS Lusitania* and *RMS Mauretania* which had both been admired for their luxury and speed. Ismay wanted three ships, which would outclass them in size, luxury and safety, but not speed.

Ismay accompanied the first of these ships, *RMS Olympic* on its maiden voyage from Southampton to New York on June 14, 1911, to ensure that all was well and worked perfectly in preparation for the next two vessels, *RMS Titanic* and *RMS Britannic*.

It was common practice for Ismay to accompany his ships on their maiden voyages, as he had done with *RMS Olympic* the year before. *Titanic's* maiden voyage was particularly important, because the ship was the pride of the White Star Line. Ismay wanted to be assured the voyage went well and that the passengers experience was of the standard White Star Line had envisaged.

According to the evidence taken on the 19 April 1912, at the U.S. Senate Inquiry into the *Titanic* disaster, Ismay stated, when questioned by Senator Smith that he boarded *Titanic* at about 9.30am as a voluntary passenger on the 10th of April, prior to her departure from Southampton at 12 o'clock.

There is no supporting evidence behind the claim that Ismay boarded *Titanic* as an Officer or a member of the crew, as suggested by the popular myth of Ismay's involvement in the ensuing events that doomed *Titanic*.

Popular folklore surrounding the disaster has it that Ismay ordered Captain Edward Smith to increase speed in an attempt to break the record for the Trans-Atlantic crossing. Apparently, this attempt was suggested to enable *Titanic* to reach New York on Tuesday, 16 April, a day before her scheduled arrival at 5,00 am Wednesday, 17 April.

In reality, *Titanic* was a brand new ship and her powerful engines had not been run in. The result of such an exercise would have been to seriously damage her engines. Some reports claim *Titanic* was travelling at 26 knots on Sunday 14 April.

Again, in reality, White Star Line's rival Cunard Line's ships *RMS Lusitania* and *RMS Mauritania* were already operating with quadruple-screw turbine drive engines, which combined economy and speed, providing a top speed of 26 knots. *Titanic* was designed for size and luxury. She operated with traditional triple-screw reciprocating steam engines and a centre-line turbine. *Titanic's* power source was definitely not "state of the art." But proven and reliable. For speed, *Titanic* was no match for *Lusitania's* and *Mauritania's* full turbine engines. *Titanic's* maximum speed was 24 knots, which meant that any record breaking attempt on the Southampton to New York speed run was, impossible.
Ismay later testified:

"I understand it has been stated that the ship was going at full speed. The ship never had been at full speed. The full speed of the ship is 78 revolutions. She works up to 80. So far as I am aware, she never exceeded 75 revolutions. She had not all her boilers on. None of the single-ended boilers were on."

"It was our intention, if we had fine weather on Monday afternoon or Tuesday, to drive the ship at full speed. That, owing to the unfortunate catastrophe, never eventuated."

During the later US and British investigations, some passengers stated they had heard Ismay talking to Captain Smith of his desire for *Titanic* to enter New York ahead of schedule and pressured Captain Smith to go faster. During the U.S. Congressional investigation, when questioned about the ships speed, Ismay testified:

Senator SMITH - "Did you have occasion to consult with the Captain about the movement of the ship?"
Mr. ISMAY - "Never."

Senator SMITH - "Did he consult you about it?"
Mr. ISMAY - "Never. Perhaps I am wrong in saying that. I should like to say this: I do not know that it was quite a matter of consulting him about it, of his consulting me about it, but what we had arranged to do was that we would not attempt to arrive in New York at the lightship before 5 o'clock on Wednesday morning."

Senator SMITH - "That was the understanding?"
Mr. ISMAY - "Yes. But that was arranged before we left Queenstown."

Senator SMITH - "Was it supposed that you could reach New York at that time without putting the ship to its full running capacity?"
Mr. ISMAY - "Oh, yes, sir. There was nothing to be gained by arriving at New York any earlier than that."

Senator SMITH - "You spoke of the revolutions on the early part of the voyage."
Mr. ISMAY - "Yes, sir."

Senator SMITH - "Those were increased as the distance was increased?"
Mr. ISMAY - "The *Titanic* being a new ship, we were gradually working her up. When you bring out a new ship you naturally do not start her running at full speed until you get everything working smoothly and satisfactorily down below."

The U S Senate inquiry concentrated on how *Titanic* sank. The British Board Of Trade inquiry concentrated on why the ship sank. Both inquiries completely cleared Ismay and White Star Line of blame. The Hearst syndicated newspapers, however, did not report either inquiry findings. The myth of J. Bruce Ismay interfering with the navigation of *Titanic* by ordering Captain E. J. Smith to proceed at a mythical top speed in order to reach New York in record time was set in stone.

CHAPTER NINE

Mystery Ship

Almost like a benediction everyone around me on the upturned boat breathed the two words, "She's gone."

- Second Officer. Charles Lightoller

Chief Officer George Stewart, began his watch close by on the Leyland Lines vessel, *Californian* at 4.00am on Monday, 15 April 1912. After realising the ship had stopped, he relieved Second officer Herbert Stone. During his briefing, Stone mentioned the ship had stopped because of ice. Stewart had retired for the night at about 9.30pm.

Between 12.00 and 1.00am Stone had also seen a ship about four or five miles off, firing white rockets. Stewart asked Stone what he did after seeing the rockets. Stone replied "As soon as she started firing the rockets, she started sailing away."

Stone did not mention he had seen five rockets, then three more, eight in total. But, did tell Stewart he had called the unknown ship up repeatedly with the Morse lamp, but got no reply. Stone also stated he had reported the ship to the Captain. Stone was asked if he thought they might be distress rockets, he said no, but had rather thought that the vessel, may have been signalling another vessel to the south of that position, out of the sight of the *Californian*.

Stewart picked up his binoculars and scouted the surrounding horizon through the early morning darkness. To the southward he spotted a steamer, displaying two masthead lights and a few lights amidships. Pointing to the ship, Stewart asked Stone if that was the ship he saw. Stone told him that it was not the same ship he had seen earlier, firing the white rockets. In fact, he did not believe he had seen that ship before.

Carpathia had reached the last known position of *Titanic* by 3.30am. Captain Rostron and his Officers were faced with nothing but water and ice around them. There were no survivors in lifeboats, no lights, no persons swimming or floating in the water, or any signs of wreckage and most of all, no *Titanic*.

After interviewing all his heads of department and making sure all preparations had been made for a large scale rescue, Rostron went to his ship's bridge. While there, he made enquiries to make certain that his orders had all being carried out. At about 3.40 am, he spotted a flare, ahead from the bow. The flare was a long way off, Rostron thought it must have been the Titanic, still afloat.

Rostron ordered *Carpathia* to proceed through the ice field. A large iceberg appeared in front, which Carpathia had to port around. Rostron continued taking precautions to ensure that his ship, on a rescue mission, did not meet the same fate as *Titanic*. He stayed well clear of anything that looked like ice.

Carpathia passed icebergs on every side, having to alter course several times to avoid them. As the ship drew closer to the source of the flare, it quickly became apparent the light was from a lifeboat, not from the great ship Rostron had heard about for its size, opulence and splendour. At 4.00am, Carpathia came close to lifeboat No 2. Another iceberg was close by. To protect the ship and the nearby lifeboat, Rostron had to starboard to get clear. Once in position with lifeboat 2 alongside, *Carpathia* was stopped.

The telephone rang for a few minutes

From the crow's nest of the pride of the White Star Line, Lookout Fleet was shocked to see the towering "blue berg" quickly rising up over the horizon. Fleet immediately telephoned the bridge to inform First Officer Murdoch of an iceberg right ahead. Unfortunately, the situation became life threateningly serious when the phone was left ringing for two to three minutes before it was answered. And, of course, by that time, it was far too late. Impact was unavoidable as the great achievement of man could not possibly avoid a collision with the mountain of ice in her path.

Was it this unanswered telephone call that sent *Titanic* to the bottom of the North Atlantic? This is the story of seamen off the ill-fated ship. Ironically, the names of these sailors, if it was sailors, if it was an individual sailor also, a name has never actually been divulged. Which is not all that surprising when dealing with myths. Names can never be given. Simply, any such information can be checked and verified.

This story fits quite nicely with rumours that circulated in 1912 and later years about events leading up to the collision and subsequent sinking of *Titanic*. However, after the wreck's discovery in 1985 by Robert Ballard from the Smiths Hole Oceanographic Institute, many of these stories and rumours have proven to be incorrect.

The Seamen's story is as follows: "It was a perfect night, clear and starlight. The sea was smooth. The temperature had dropped to freezing Sunday morning. We knew or believed that the cold was due to the nearness of bergs, but we had not even run against cake ice up to the time the ice mountain loomed up. *Titanic* raced through a calm sea in which there was no ice into the berg that sank her."

"The First Officer of the watch was Murdoch. He was on the bridge. Captain Smith may have been near at hand, but he was not visible to us who were about to wash the decks.

Hitchens, quartermaster, was at the wheel. Fleet was the outlook."

"Fleet reported the berg, but the telephone was not answered on the bridge at once. A few minutes later, the telephone call was answered, but it was too late."

"It was 11.40 P.M. Sunday, April 14. Struck an iceberg. The iceberg was very dark and about 250 feet in height."

"The *Titanic* struck the berg a glancing blow on the starboard bow. The ship, which was traveling between twenty and twenty-three knots an hour, crashed into the berg at a point about forty feet back to the stern."

"*Titanic's* bottom was torn away to about the forebridge. The tear was fully fifty feet in length and below the water line."

Already, there are a few discrepancies between the story and the actual events, leading up to the disaster. First, The source of the story states that the temperature had dropped to freezing on Sunday morning. Sunday April 14 1912, however, began remarkably mild for April. Many of the passengers including Colonel Archibald Gracie testified, they had been enjoying the sun throughout the morning. The temperature had continued to drop during the afternoon, to freezing by Sunday night. *Titanic's* Marconi room had continued to receive berg warnings throughout the day of Sunday

April 14. *Titanic* was 50 nautical miles away from the reported ice field by 7.30 pm.

It was general knowledge after the rescue ship *Carpathia* arrived in New York with *Titanic's* surviving passengers and crew that Frederick Fleet was the lookout person that alerted Murdoch on the ships bridge of the looming peril, prior to collision. Also present in the crows-nest was Reginald Lee.

But that was not publicised in most news papers and other news sources of the time. The source of this story only mentions Fleet as being on lookout at 11.40 P.M. on Sunday 14 April.

"*Titanic's* bottom was torn away to about the forebridge. The tear was fully fifty feet in length and below the water line". This statement indicates a huge gash below the water line of the ships massive hull. This was the subject of some conjecture between 1912 and 1985 before the wreck of *Titanic* was finally discovered, along with notions that the ship sank intact or the ship broke in two, prior to its final plunge to the bottom of the North Atlantic Ocean.

 After the expedition to the wreck site, visible evidence was produced proving the ship was sunk by a series of rivets popping from seams in her hull from the pressure provided from the collision, to a maximum length of 245 feet, opening five of her sixteen water tight compartments to the Atlantic Ocean.

The story continues: "Murdoch, after the ship struck the berg, gave orders to put the helm hard to port and the ship hit the berg again."

"Afterwards Murdoch gave an order to the carpenter to sound the wells to learn how much water the ship was taking in. The carpenter came up and told Murdoch the *Titanic* had seven feet of water in her in less than seven minutes."

"Then Captain Smith, who had put in an appearance, gave orders to get the boats ready."

"There was less than ten minutes between the time *Titanic* first struck the berg and the second crash. Both of which brought big pieces of ice showering down on the ship."

"Orders came to the crew to stand by the boats. The boats were got out. There were twenty-two boats all told."

Visible evidence of the stern of *Titanic* since its discovery in 1985 indicates no damage from the berg towards the stern of the ship. Murdoch's order to "Hard to port," prevented any further damage to *Titanic* from the collision with the berg.

No other witness evidence claims the ship hit with the berg a second or third time.

Evidence from Second Officer Lightoller and quartermaster Hitchens both stated Captain Smith gave orders to the ships carpenter to sound the ship, not Murdoch.

Titanic's total lifeboat number was twenty boats. 14 standard lifeboats, 2 emergency cutters and 4 collapsible boats. Not the stated 22 in this story. The stated number of lifeboats may have been as a result of the confusion evident prior to *Carpathia's* arrival into New York, when news about the disaster were sketchy, to say the least.

The story continues: "Ismay, with his two daughters and a millionaire, Sir Cosmo Duff-Gordon, and the latter's family, got into the first accident or emergency boats, which are about twenty-eight feet long, and were ready for lowering under the bridge. The boat in which Ismay and Sir Cosmo left were manned by seven seamen. There were seventeen persons in that boat."

"This boat pulled away from the ship a half hour before any of the lifeboats were put into the water. There were thirteen first-class passengers and five sailors in the emergency boat. Both boats were away from the ship within ten or fifteen minutes of the ship crashing into the berg."

This is a strange part of the story as no survivor testimony or evidence supports this twist of the tale. Certainly no mention of Ismay's daughters, Margaret and Evelyn being onboard *Titanic* during her maiden voyage is mentioned in the list of passengers or crew and no mention from survivors indicates the presence of Ismay's daughters being onboard. History has also never substantiated this claim.

This section of the story is certainly worthy of a modern day conspiracy theory of an attempted cover-up from the senior Officers of *Titanic*, while attempting to protect the most important dignitaries onboard the ship in her most perilous mishap.

The first boat launched from *Titanic* was in fact a standard lifeboat 7 from the starboard side, supervised by Murdoch, assisted by Third Officer Herbert Pitman, Fifth Officer Harold Lowe and White Star Line chairman, Ismay. The first boat away did not leave until 12.45 am, over an hour after the collision, not the stated ten or fifteen minutes. The emergency cutter lifeboats could carry a maximum of forty persons, not the stated sixty. The standard lifeboats however could hold a capacity of sixty-five persons and even the collapsibles could hold a maximum of forty-seven persons each. The Duff-Gordon's actually evacuated the *Titanic* on boat 1, which was the emergency cutter from the starboard side, which was the fifth lifeboat to launch from the stricken liner at 1.05 am, with ten other occupants.

J. Bruce Ismay stayed onboard *Titanic*, assisting with the loading on the starboard side, before leaving the sinking ship on collapsible C at 2.00 am, after exhaustively checking and ensuring that there were no other women and children on the starboard side nearby.

~ ~ ~ ~

As the survivors from the first lifeboat were climbing aboard *Carpathia* at 4.10am. daylight was dawning. All around them the horror of the events that had occurred over the past few hours became apparent. The remaining lifeboats became visible, within an area of about 4 miles or 6 kilometres.

About 20 icebergs surrounded the vessel, varying in size from 150 to 200 feet high with numerous smaller growlers, ranging between 10 to 12 feet high by 10 to 15 feet long. It seemed incredible to *Carpathia's* crew their ship had successfully avoided so many icebergs, Rostron was amazed they hadn't hit any of them. He later commented to a close friend, Captain Barr, also of the Cunard Line "When day broke, I saw the ice I had steamed through during the night, I shuddered, and could only think that some other hand than mine was on the helm during the night."

Rostron remained on the bridge as *Titainic's* survivors came aboard. He asked for the officer in charge of the first lifeboat - Fourth Officer Boxhall - to come to the bridge.

Still suffering from exposure from the cold and shivering in front of Rostron, Boxhall explained how *Titanic* had sunk about 2.30am. His voice broke when he told Rostron about the hundreds of people, maybe a thousand or more, who had gone down with the ship, as they could not possibly have survived the icy cold water.

The toll of the sinking surprised Rostron, maybe it was emotion that caused him to pause a few moments after hearing about the number of victims. He finally replied, "Thank you mister, go below and get some coffee and try to get warm".
Stewart spoke to Captain Lord of the *Californian*, at 4.30am, mentioning that the second officer had said he

had seen rockets, during the middle watch. Lord replied "Oh yes I know, he had been telling me."

Both Lord and Stewart proceeded to the bridge, where Stewart pointed out the ship he had pointed out to Stone. Lord was preparing to start the ship, to proceed through the ice to continue their voyage. Stone asked Lord if he was going to find out why the other ship had been firing rockets. Lord replied "No, she looks all right; she is not making signals now". Stewart had not told the Captain that Stone did not believe it was the same ship he had been watching through the night. Stewart made a quick check of the ships scrap logbook to discover that Stone had not made any mention of the white rockets he had observed from the ship south of their position, overnight.

At 5.15am *Californian* got under way. She began very slowly as the ship was still surrounded with the ice that had menaced them the night before, causing them to stop overnight.

At 5.40am Chief Officer George Stewart entered the cabin of *Californian* wireless operator Cyril Evans, saying "There's a ship been firing rockets". Then asking, "Will you see if you can find out whether there is anything the matter?"

This information startled Evans, he immediately jumped out of his bunk, quickly slipped on a pair of trousers and slippers, then applied his headphones at once. He listened to find out if anyone was transmitting, but he could not hear anything, so he sent out a CQ message.

The Canadian Pacific vessel, *Mount Temple* answered his general call, saying "Do you know the *Titanic* has struck an iceberg, and she is sinking", giving Evans *Titanic's* position. Evans was hardly able to gather his thoughts, when the German steamer, *Frankfurt* jumped in, informing Evans of the same horrifying news and again giving the position of the stricken liner.

Cyril Evans had written down *Titanic's* position. Then handed it to Stewart, who then left the room to notify Captain Lord at about 5.50am. Evans then contacted the *Virginian*, of the Allan Line. The *Virginian* gave *Titanic's* position of 41.46 North, 50.14 West, saying "she is sinking, passengers in boats". Throughout these transmissions, Evans was aware that the *Frankfurt, Virginian* and a Russian liner *Birma* were sailing to the position to give assistance, although Evans had no idea how far from *Titanic's* reported position these vessels were.

The *Frankfurt* had passed *Californian* on her way to Europe earlier the day before, but how far east of *Titanic's* position, Evans did not know. The *Virginian* was coming from the direction of Cape Race, but he did not know their position at the time of transmission. He did know however, that his equipment had a maximum range between 100 and 240 miles.

By 6.10am the *Californian* was sailing the 19 to 20 miles to the last position of *Titanic*. Evans had not heard anything from *Carpathia* until about 8.30 when they arrived at the position, alongside *Carpathia*.

Thirty year old secretary from London, Laura Mabel Francatelli, later recalled her joy at seeing *Carpathia* arrive at the disaster scene "Oh at daybreak, when we saw the lights of that ship, about 4 miles away, we rowed like mad, & passed icebergs like mountains, at last about 6:30 the dear *Carpathia* picked us up, our little boat was like a speck against that giant. Then came my weakest moment, they lowered a rope swing, which was awkward to sit on with my life preserver 'round me. Then they hauled me up by the side of the boat. Can you imagine, swinging in the air over the sea, I just shut my eyes & clung tight saying 'Am I safe?' at last I felt a strong arm pulling me onto the boat."

Survivors on lifeboat 13 started boarding at 6.30am. Among them was Second Class passenger, Lawrence Beesley. Being a science teacher, Beesley was sceptical about superstitions. This scepticism reflected in a comment from him "I shall never say again that 13 is an unlucky number. Boat 13 is the best friend we ever had."

Over the next few hours, boatload after boatload of survivors came alongside and boarded *Carpathia*. Many of her passengers were aware that something was happening and wanted to take a look, so lined the side rails of the decks to watch the boats and the people coming aboard. As the survivors came aboard, they were separated into their various Classes, names were taken, medical checks were carried out. Then the survivor was escorted to the relevant dining saloon and given hot coffee, soup and sandwiches and if required, whiskey and brandy. All the lifeboats were hauled onboard, except for the upturned and damaged collapsible boats, which were abandoned.

Left - Titanic survivors coming aboard Carpathia, Right - Titanic lifeboat hauled aboard.

Middle top - Collapsible B with survivors. Middle bottom - lifeboats coming alongside Carpathia

Rostron was impressed with the way his crew carried out their duties and followed his orders so precisely throughout the entire rescue operation. He was also amazed with the behaviour of *Titanic's* survivors. He always remembered the orderly way in which the survivors boarded *Carpathia*, With the exception of one woman, there were no anxiety displays - in fact the survivors boarded *Carpathia* in complete silence. Rostron noticed the many survivors who were hardly wearing anything and imagined how quickly they had to abandon *Titanic*.

The last survivors to board *Carpathia* did so at 8.30am. For those in greatest need, *Carpathia's* own First Class passengers gave up their cabins. The most prominent guests being Mrs Astor, Mrs Widener and Mrs Thayer, who were assigned to the Captains quarters. All in all, there were an extra 705 passengers onboard *Carpathia*.

Throughout the rescue process, as each boat came alongside, those already onboard waited eagerly as more boarded to see if their loved ones were included. A few scenes of joy erupted as some were reunited. As the process continued, many came to the realisation that there would be no reunion, as their loved ones had perished.

Rostron was now faced with another decision, where to take the survivors. The ship's doctor, McGhee, was examining White Star Lines president, J. Bruce Ismay. It is believed that Ismay may have been suffering from an anxiety breakdown after the sinking of *Titanic*. Rostron asked Ismay, his impression on where to take the survivors. Ismay left that decision up to Rostron.

The Azores would have been the better decision, but according to Rostron, the survivors had been through enough already and needed to disembark as soon as possible and, in any case, *Carpathia* did not have enough provisions to last a voyage to the Azores. Nova Scotia was closer, but Rostron, worried about the extra passengers, decided that the ordeal of travelling through much more ice may be detrimental to their wellbeing.

RMS Olympic sent a wireless message, suggesting they be transferred to her, but again, Rostron believed they did not need the ordeal of being transferred to another vessel, also, *Olympic* was *Titanic's* sister ship, Rostron believed the survivors would have hideous memories brought to mind if they were expected to transfer to *Olympic*. After conversing again with Ismay, Rostron believed it had to be New York. New York was the most expensive option for the Cunard Line. It was also the best option for the survivors.

First Officer William Murdoch shot himself

William McMaster Murdoch was born in February 1873 into a seafaring family, to Captain Samuel Murdoch and Jane Muirhead McMaster, at Dalbeattie, Dumfries and Galloway, Scotland. Murdoch was educated at the old Dalbeattie Primary School, then at Dalbeattie High School in Alpine Street, where Murdoch became top in his class for mathematics, gaining his diploma in 1887.

Following School, William Murdoch began his seafaring career. He served his apprenticeship at William, Joyce and Coy in Liverpool. In the fourth year of his five year apprenticeship, Murdoch was confident enough to pass his Second Mates Certificate in his first attempt, while serving on the *Charles Cosworth*, a 1079 ton Bargue from Liverpool.

In 1892, Murdoch joined the *Iquiqe* as Second Officer with his father, Samuel Murdoch as commander on a voyage that would last 18 months from Rotterdam to Frederikstad in Sweden, then Capetown, Newcastle, Antofagasta and Iquiqe. In 1895 Murdoch gained his First Mates Certificate on the *Saint Guthbert*, sailing from Ipswich to Mauritius to Newport in Wales via Newcastle, Callao and Hamburg.

Murdoch gained his Extra Masters Certificate No. 025780 at the age of 23 on his first attempt, gaining the privilege of obtaining the highest British Board Of Trade Certificates within the shortest possible time. As a comparison, both *Titanic's* Captain Edward John Smith and Chief Officer Henry Wilde failed their Extra Masters Certificates on their first attempt.

During the Boer War, Murdoch trained as a Lieutenant in the Royal Navy Reserve, qualifying him to join White Star Line, as a steam ship officer in 1899. Between 1899 and 1912, Murdoch served on many White Star Line vessels, gradually rising in rank from Fourth Officer to First Officer. First, the first luxury ship, *Medic*, where Murdoch became friends with Charles Lightoller on the Australia run. Murdoch became third officer in 1900.

William Murdoch joined the *Runic* in 1901, also on the Australia run, becoming Second Officer, and becoming popular among his colleagues, gaining the reputation of the "best and smartest sailor afloat". While aboard the *Runic*, in 1903, Murdoch met a New Zealand School teacher, 29 year old, Ada Florence Banks, beginning a long distance correspondence relationship.

Also in 1903, Murdoch entered the North-Atlantic run, joining the *Arabic*, as Second Officer. During *Arabic's* maiden voyage, Murdoch overturned his Captain's order by narrowly averting serious danger, when another ship was spotted bearing down on *Arabic*. Murdoch, displaying his quick thinking and cool head, rushed into the Wheel House, brushing aside the Quartermaster and steered his vessel straight ahead, after his superior Officer, Fox, had ordered "hard-a-port". The two ships passed within inches of one another. *Arabic's* Captain Jones later remarked, how impressed he was with Murdoch's action. Any alteration in course at that moment would have resulted in disaster.

Murdoch became the First Officer on board the *Celtic* in 1904, which was the largest ship afloat in 1901, and the first of the Big Liners, with a gross tonnage of 21,035. Murdoch also made two voyages with the International Mercantile's America Line, onboard the former White Star Lines' *Germanic*, during 1904, with Captain Bartlett.

Murdoch rejoined his friend Charles Lightoller on the *Oceanic* in January 1905 to February 1906. *Oceanic* as the first White Star Line vessel to suffer a mutiny. According to an article in the *New York Times* on October 12, 1905, 35 stokers were imprisoned, after complaining about their working conditions and accommodation.

Serving on *Cedric* for two voyages, Murdoch was First Officer from February 1906 to May 9 1906. He then transferred to the *Teutonic* for three voyages as part of his training for his service in the Royal Naval Reserve - as the *Teutonic* was armed. After serving again on the *Cedric* as Second Officer, he then rejoined *Oceanic* as First Officer on May 9, 1906.

William Murdoch, at 34 years old married Ada Florence Banks, who was 33 years old, on September 2, 1907 at St. Denys Church in Southampton. They made their home at 94 Belmont Road, Southampton - now 116 Belmont Road.

According to *The London Gazette* on September 10, 1909, Murdoch was promoted from Sub-Lieutenant to Lieutenant in the Royal Naval Reserve on 8 September 1909. In May 1911, he was sent to Belfast, Northern Ireland, to join White Star Line's newest and largest ship, *Olympic*. Murdoch was known to be a "canny and dependable man" by the time he joined *Olympic* in May 1911.

Olympic, the first of the new Olympic-Class superliners of the White Star Line, was designed and built to outclass the Cunard Lines *Lusitania* and *Mauritania*, sacrificing speed for sheer size and luxury. At 45,324 gross registered tons, *Olympic* required the finest crew White Star Line could muster.

Captain E. J. Smith assembled the crew, including Henry Wilde as Chief Officer, William Murdoch as First Officer and Henry McElroy as Chief Purser. Leaving Southampton on June 14, 1911, Olympic began her maiden voyage to New York.

Olympic's fifth voyage to New York had to be abandoned on September 20, after her hull was severely damaged in a collision with the Royal Navy Cruiser, *HMS Hawke*. *Olympic* had to return to Belfast for six weeks of repairs, which delayed the completion of the second Olympic Class vessels - *Titanic*.

The incident between *HMS Hawke* and *Olympic* was a financial disaster for White Star Line, as White Star's insurance company, Lloyds Of London, refused to pay insurance claims for the damage. Murdoch rejoined *Olympic* on December 11, 1911.

Two more incidents further marred *Olympic's* career. In March 1912, *Olympic* struck a sunken vessel and lost a propeller, further delaying the completion of *Titanic*, then she nearly ran aground while leaving Belfast on her way back to Southampton.

Soon after these incidents, Murdoch received the news that he was to join the larger newer vessel of the Class - *Titanic*.

Following *Titanic's* sinking, there were many reports that First Officer William Murdoch had committed suicide on the boat deck, before she sank beneath the surface. These claims seem to be mere rumour as contradicting accounts were presented by surviving passengers and crew.

Many newspaper reports contained quotes from "Anonymous" witnesses, indicating they may have been fabricated stories, while many other accounts claimed that another Officer, other than Murdoch, committed suicide. Still other reports and accounts state that Murdoch shot himself at different times throughout the lifeboat launching and eventual sinking, while yet others claim that Captain Smith shot himself and some claim that it was Chief Officer Henry Wilde who shot himself.

Second Officer Charles Lightoller was a good friend of Murdoch and highly respected him. He worked beside

Murdoch onboard *Arabic* on the occasion that Murdoch averted a serious collision. A letter that Lightoller sent to Ada Murdoch from New York on Aril 24 1912, on behalf of himself and the other surviving Officers - Fourth Officer G. Groves Boxhall, Third Officer H. J. Pitman, and Fifth Officer H. G. Lowe - expressing their disgust at the reports of Murdoch's suicide. The letter reads as follows
:
"Dear Mrs. Murdoch,

I am writing on behalf of the surviving officers to express our deep sympathy in this, your awful loss. Words cannot convey our feelings, - much less a letter. I deeply regret that I missed communicating with you by last mail to refute the reports that were spread in the newspapers. I was practically the last man, and certainly the last officer, to see Mr. Murdoch. He was then endeavouring to launch the starboard forward collapsible boat. I had already got mine from off the top of our quarters. You will understand when I say that I was working the port side of the ship, and Mr. Murdoch was principally engaged on the starboard side of the ship, filling and launching the boats. Having got my boat down off the top of the house, and there being no time to open it, I left it and ran across to the starboard side, still on top of the quarters. I was then practically looking down on your husband and his men. He was working hard, personally assisting, overhauling the forward boat's fall. At this moment the ship dived, and we were all in the water. Other reports as to the ending are absolutely false. Mr. Murdoch died like a man, doing his duty. Call on us without hesitation for anything we can do for you."

"Yours very sincerely".

Signed C. H. Lightoller."

Ada Murdoch authorised the letter to be published in *The Dumfries & Galloway Standard & Advertiser,* on May 11, 1912.

Wireless operator Harold Bride also claims that Murdoch died after *Titanic* sank, from hypothermia. In 1954, Bride told maritime historian Mr. Ernest Robinson:

"They had been part of a group trying to launch the forward starboard collapsible lifeboat, normally stored on the roof of the officers' quarters. Bride initially on Port side, assisting with Collapsible B. This falls bottom-up on the boat-deck. Bride goes round to Collapsible A over the deck-housing. Bride is near Murdoch, who is helping to sort Collapsible A. Bridge goes under, boat deck engulfed, Murdoch and Bride are both swept off the boat-deck and into the sea. Some men are swimming towards Collapsible A, which has floated off. The forward funnel stays part with sounds like gunshots as the funnel sways forwards and to starboard and crashes down on those swimming near Collapsible A. That boat is swamped, those in it hurled out, as it is moved farther away off the starboard side. Bride is on the wrong side of the funnel and is swept towards the centreline of the submerged bow section, now sinking" "more rapidly. Like Lightoller, he is sucked down, but unlike Lightoller he comes up under the still-capsized

Collapsible B. B is there because of being sucked sideways towards the centreline of the sinking ship."

"After a time of great fear, Bride manages to emerge from under Collapsible B and hangs onto its side. Later he reaches the top when people help him up, by then the Titanic had gone under. In the sea, Bride sees Murdoch clinging to a deck chair but already dead, Moody is by his side, also dead."

~ ~ ~ ~

A wireless message was sent to the *Californian*, floating nearby, announcing Rostron's decision to sail to New York "I am taking the survivors to New York. Please stay in the vicinity and pick up any bodies". Before proceeding, Rostron wanted *Carpathia* to cruise around the wreck site, to ensure all who could be picked up had been plucked out of the icy waters.

Navigating through the debris field, *Carpathia* passed many small items of wreckage, deck-chairs, cushions, empty lifebelts and several white pilasters, but nothing distinctive, except one body floating on the surface. Realising nothing more could be done, Rostron plotted his course to New York.

Continuing to do all he could for the survivors, Rostron arranged a short memorial service for all those who had had their dreams washed away - the wives, husbands, sons, daughters, uncles and aunts, grandmothers and grandfathers, who perished in the water, leaving nothing but icebergs and growlers as grave markers.

An Episcopalian clergyman, Reverend Anderson, gave thanks and paid respects to the lost, watched by the people of *Titanic* and *Carpathia*. As final prayers were being said at 8.50am, *Carpathia* steamed over the grave of *Titanic*. Then, set out full steam ahead for New York.

Top Left Cunard Lines Carpathia, Top Right, Leyland Lines Californian.

Centre Left, Titanic Survivors on deck of Carpathia. Centre Right Captain Arthur Rostron.

Bottom Left, Titanic Lifebelt, Bottom Right Titanic survivors onboard Carpathia.

Again, Rostron went below to check J. Bruce Ismay, who was lodged in Doctor McGhee's cabin. He suggested he may need to send a wireless message forward to New York, informing them of the disaster. Ismay agreed and wrote "Deeply regret advise you *Titanic* sank this morning after collision with iceberg, resulting in serious loss of life. Full particulars later." After asking Rostron's opinion, the message was sent.

Rostron realised the severity of Ismay's condition. Ismay seemed overcome with grief and shock at the tragedy, seeming to be very emotional, he was barely talking to anyone and if he did talk, he wasn't saying much and more alarmingly, he was refusing to eat anything much. Rostron placed Ismay in the continuing care of Dr McGhee, ordering he to be left alone in peace. Ismay remained in the Doctor's cabin for the entire journey to New York.

For the next few days, before reached New York, Rostron had declared a news freeze from *Carpathia*. He insisted the wireless set would be used only for official messages and private messages from *Titanic* survivors only. During this time, frantic messages were received from land stations demanding further information about the disaster. Rostron ordered they be ignored, even messages from U.S President Taft. Rostron wanted to avoid any chances of false information being transmitted.

The news blackout from *Carpathia* attracted the attention of America's most influential newsman. William Randolph Hearst. The owner of Americas largest newspaper chain.

Hearst had a long standing hatred for White Star Line, in particular, J. Bruce Ismay, since Ismay refused to co operate with him over two decades earlier, while Ismay was a White Star Line agent based in New York. Hearst saw the *Titanic* disaster, and the fact that Ismay survived, to run a scathing campaign against Ismay in retaliation for his non co-operation, That retaliation formed the foundation of Hearst's systematic newspaper campaign that would haunt Ismay for the rest of his life.

Before *Carpathia* reached New York, many rumours surrounding the disaster were brewing, as news was sketchy at best. Many survivors were sending messages to relatives and loved ones. As these messages were being picked up on land based stations, they were forwarded on to New York and England. Any snippet of news about the disaster included in these messages, were forwarded onto news agencies.

One rumour was adapted from a single word by the vice president of *Titanic's* owners, the International Mercantile Marine Company, Philip Franklin, who stated about the disaster "I thought her unsinkable, and I based my opinion on the best expert advice available. I don't understand it". The single word, being "unsinkable" was immediately picked up by the media, who ran the quote as claiming, "White Star said *Titanic* is 'unsinkable". Thus generating the myth that exists today.

A further message sent from *Carpathia* helped to seal Ismay's fate with his nemesis in America and a Senator. The message "Most desirable *Titanic* crew aboard *Carpathia* should be returned home earliest moment possible. Suggest you hold *Cedric*, sailing daylight

Friday unless you see any reason contrary. Propose returning in her myself. Please send outfit of clothes, including shoes, for me to *Cedric*. Have nothing of my own. Please Reply. Yamsi". The name Yamsi is Ismay in reverse.

Top - The Officers of Carpathia, surround Captain Rostron.

Bottom - The surviving Officers of Titanic - Back left to right - Fifth Officer Harold Lowe, Second Officer Charles Lightoller, Fourth Officer Joseph Boxhall. Seated - Third Officer Herbert Pittman.

Senator William Smith urged the Senate to investigate the sinking of *Titanic*. He was granted that approval and a Senate sub-committee, headed by Smith himself, was set up.

Smith knew if Ismay and the crew were to return to England, it could become problematic for them to return to the US at a later date, so Senator Smith boarded a train to New York. He soon realised his fear was unfounded, as Ismay was more than willing to co-operate.

The same could not be said about Ismay's arch enemy, W Randolph Hearst, who believed the message from Ismay to be some kind of code. If Ismay wanted to leave the US for England as soon as possible, then obviously Ismay had something to hide.

So the story of Ismay ordering Captain E.J. Smith to break the trans-Atlantic speed record, thus causing the *Titanic* disaster, was born. That story was reinforced after *Carpathia* docked in New York, as several First-Class passengers, while making insurance claims, used the story to bolster their claims.

One such claim was made by First Class passenger Elizabeth Lines, who stated at the Senate inquiry that she overheard a comment from Ismay during a two hour conversation with Captain Smith on Saturday 13 April: "We will beat the *Olympic* and get into New York on Tuesday". It is not absolutely clear what she meant by that comment. *RMS Olympic* was in the North-Atlantic at that time. But, was on her return voyage from New York to Southampton at the time of the disaster, not Southampton to New York. So, it's not known if Lines thought the *Olympic* was also sailing to New York at that time, if Ismay was hoping to beat *Olympic* into New York, or not. In any case, *RMS Olympic* had at no time held any speed record from Europe to the US, or vice versa.

Captain Rostron's decision to order the news blackout was also blamed on Ismay as numerous newspapers around the world went to print.

For instance *The Bendigo Advertiser*, a newspaper in Victoria, Australia, wrote on Saturday April 20, 1912 - indicating how slowly news travelled in 1912 - "It is thought Mr. Joseph Bruce Ismay, managing director of the White Star Line, who is among the rescued passengers on board the *Carpathia*, has used his influence to prevent the transmission of news". The comment here, also reflected many articles about the lack of news coming from *Carpathia*, was contained in the Hearst syndicated newspapers, throughout the United States. Hearst continued to blame all aspects of the *Titanic* disaster, squarely on White Star Lines president, J. Bruce Ismay.

CHAPTER TEN

New York, New York

To my poor fellow-sufferers: My heart overflows with grief for you all and is laden with sorrow that you are weighed down with this terrible burden that has been thrust upon us. May God be with us and comfort us all.

- Eleanor Smith - wife of the late Captain Edward J. Smith.

As the news blackout from *Carpathia* continued, until her arrival in New York, the rumours and concern from others extended to the top office of the United States. President Taft was becoming increasingly worried about his military aid, friend and *Titanic* passenger, Colonel Archibald Butt. Communication stations along the coast had failed to get any response from the *Carpathia* from the day *Titanic* foundered.

On April 16, President Taft ordered the Chester Class Cruisers, *USS. Salem* and *USS. Chester,* from Boston. *Salem* and *Chester's* orders were to sail to the scene of the disaster and send back any information they could to determine what had happened. Taft had also tentatively considered sending the two cutters, *USS. Seneca* and *USS. Mohawk,* from New York, to proceed to Sandy Hook to rendezvous with *Carpathia*, to act as an escort into New York.

US. Secretary McVeagh considered the possibility of sending the Cutter *USS Gresham,* to also rendezvous with *Carpathia*, with the idea of carrying newspaper journalists to board *Carpathia* to get information direct from the survivors and then to send the information direct to Naval Communications stations. Who, in turn, would release the information as it was received. Unfortunately for McVeagh, this plan would require cooperation from Cunard Line in granting the journalists permission to board *Carpathia*. McVeagh was forced to abandon the plan when Cunard refused to cooperate, continuing Rostron's plan to protect *Titanic's* survivors for as long as possible. Certainly for as long as they are aboard his vessel.

Meanwhile, the weather from the wreck site to New York had changed considerably. *Carpathia* had sailed through fog, rain and scattered thunder-storms over the last four days, this weather-pattern continued as *Carpathia* approached the City of New York.

Reports from the Nantucket Shoal Lightship stated that *Carpathia* had passed by at 6 am on April 18. Estimates put her arrival at Cunard's Pier 54 at approximately 9.00pm, although no one in New York was certain, because of Rostrons continued news blackout. Snippets of information had reached authorities from messages sent from survivors to loved ones. Still, no one knew for certain.

Everything about *Carpathia*, before her entry into New York on 18 April 1912, would have made a fantastic thriller novel today. Prior to her docking at Cunard's Pier 54, *Carpathia* was the Mystery Ship.

Many imaginary tales were circulating globally. Articles of news were varying day to day. Such as: many of the lifeboats - full of survivors were sucked under as the great ship sank, all the passengers are safe and transferred to lifeboats, the women survivors were going insane through grief of the loss of husbands, many other ships had picked up further survivors and, *Titanic* was under tow to Halifax, the *Baltic* had picked up a further 250 survivors, before her arrival in New York.

What is true is that before her arrival in New York, *Carpathia* had become known as 'The Ship Of Sorrows' and 'The Ship Of Widows.'

The world wanted to know what had happened, who was to blame and in accordance with tradition, who the hero was. The largest newspaper chain in America, owned by Hearst, had already decided who the villain was - Ismay. There was only one character needed. Every tragic story needs that knight in shining armour, who comes to the aid of the damsel in distress, Right? As the wireless of *Carpathia* remained silent, speculation was growing to unparalleled heights.

A selection of Newspaper headlines, giving a variety of descriptions of the Titanic disaster.

Journalists were frantically trying to get the scoop about the disaster, jostling to be the reporter who got the latest news. Every avenue of news gathering were exhausted. No news was coming from the *Carpathia* herself. Another source was desperately needed. That main source would be the survivors themselves.

Throughout the day of *Carpathia's* arrival, newsmen were frantically trying to get a vantage point as close to the ship's point of arrival as they could, to get that scoop over all the other newsmen present. Their luck turned sour as Cunard refused to give them entry passes onto Pier 54, insisting on reserving the Pier for relatives of the survivors only. Security around the Pier was stepped up to prevent unauthorized persons entry onto the pier.

The weather conditions were not friendly to the waiting media. Thick fog throughout the day was causing the press to speculate the arrival of *Carpathia* could be delayed until around 1.00am the next day.

The Hero - Captain E.J. Smith

Born on January 27, 1850 to Edward and Catherine Smith in Hanley, Staffordshire. Edward John Smith attended Etruria British School, until the age of 13. Moving to Liverpool at age 17, he became an apprentice on the ship *Senator Weber*, which was owned by A. Gibson & Co. of Liverpool.

On January 13 1887, E. J Smith married Sarah Eleanor Pennington in Winwick, Cheshire. Their daughter Helen Melville Smith was born in Waterloo, Liverpool on April 2 1898. The family lived in Highfield, Southampton.

In March 1880, Smith joined White Star Line as Fourth Officer on the *RMS Cedric*. Serving on the companies' liners to Australia and New York. He rose quickly in status. In 1887, Smith received his first command, on the *Republic*. Earning his Extra Masters Certificate in 1888, he became a Full Lieutenant with the Royal Naval Reserve, allowing his ship the distinction, as a British merchant vessel, of flying the Blue Ensign of the R.N.R.

In 1895, Smith's second command was with *Majestic* for nine years. Transported troops to the Cape Colony during the Boer War, without incident, earning him the reputation as a "safe Captain", for which he earned the Transport Medal, given to him by King Edward VII in 1903. Smith also became known as the "Millionaires Captain" because England's Upper-Class preferred to sail on ships under his command.

Smith commanded White Star Lines newest ships from 1904, with his first, the biggest vessel in the world at that time, *Baltic*. Her maiden voyage on June 29 1904 from Liverpool to New York was without incident. After three years, Smith was assigned the big ship, *Adriatic*, her maiden voyage also going without incident. While with the *Adriatic*, Smith received the Royal Naval Reserve's Long Service Medal. By virtue of this award, he was now entitled to be addressed as, Captain Edward John Smith, R.D. (Reserve Decoration), R.N.R. (Royal Naval Reserve).

As the most experienced Captain in the White Star fleet and one of the most experienced in the world, E. J.

Smith was asked to command the first of the new generation super-liners, that of *RMS Olympic*. The maiden voyage again went without incident, until reaching New York on June 21, 1911. While docking at Pier 59, one of the twelve tugs maneuvering *Olympic* into he berth became jammed under her stern, before working itself free.

Another incident occurred with *Olympic* on September 20, 1911. Smith was on the bridge when his ships shear size is believed to have caused the Royal Navy cruiser, *HMS Hawke* to be sucked into *Olympic's* hull. The collision caused damage to one of her propeller shafts, while filling two of her compartments with water. The Royal Navy warship lost her prow. An inquiry by the Royal Navy found *Olympic* was to blame for the incident. On arrival at Harland and Wolff for repairs, *Titanic's* finishing had to be halted so that a propeller shaft could be used to replace *Olympic's* damaged one. In February 1912 *Olympic* lost a propeller. *Titanic's* completion was delayed again, so that a propeller could be removed and installed on *Olympic*. This incident put *Titanic's* maiden voyage back, from March 20 to April 10.

One myth is that Captain E. J. Smith was set to retire after the maiden voyage of *Titanic*. An article in *The Halifax Morning Chronicle* on April 9, 1912, stated that Smith would remain in command of *Titanic* "until the Company - White Star Line completed a larger and finer steamer" - believed to be *RMS Britannic*.

Although history has seen Smith in a favorable light, many questions still remain about Smith's adequacy.

The fate of so many passengers and crew were firmly at the hands of Captain E. J. Smith. Any ship's Captain takes full responsibility for the performance of his vessel, full responsibility for her crew and the safety of her passengers. The events of the night of 14 to 15 April 1912, including the loss of the ship, passengers and crew falls completely with Captain Smith. It was Captain Smith who ignored the ice warnings throughout the day and night of April 14, who failed to adequately order a lifeboat drill for the voyage from Southampton to New York, who failed to order an abandon ship, failed to ensure the lifeboats were full before launching and failed to ensure the rockets were fired in the correct order, as set out according to the Laws Of The Sea. The Captain is always ultimately responsible for his ship.

What happened to Smith?

Just what did happen to Captain Smith? Many contradicting stories circulated after *Titanic's* sinking. The popular belief is that he entered the bridge, then closed the door and calmly sank out of sight as the great ship slid beneath the surface. This scenario sounds simplistic and follows the popular belief of how a hero should die. Calm, decisive and, in Smith's case, not forgetting the British "Stiff Upper Lip."

The mystery of Captain Smith will remain a subject for conjecture, as his body was never found. A childhood friend would later say "Ted Smith passed away just as he would love to do. To stand on the bridge of the vessel and go down with her is characteristic of all his actions when we were boys together."

An unnamed witness claimed that Smith shouted "Be British boys. Be British!" before going under with the ship. An "unnamed" witness always lays the groundwork for fiction.

Named witnesses however claimed contradicting accounts. The majority of the witness accounts all follow one theme. That Captain Smith was washed overboard as the forward section of the ship was engulfed by the ocean.

G.A. Drayton claimed Smith had simply been washed off the bridge as *Titanic* lunged forward, saying: "I saw him swim back to the sinking ship. He went down with it, in my sight."

Seaman G. A. Hogg said: "I saw Captain Smith in the water alongside a raft. 'There's the Skipper, I yelled. Give him a hand'. They did, but he shook himself free and shouted to us 'Goodbye boys, I'm going to follow the ship."

Other witnesses claimed differing variations of this scenario with some claiming Smith saved a child before returning to his ship. One such variation came from Entree Cook, H. Maynard, who stated that while on a lifeboat, he saw Captain Smith swim up to them and hand over a baby before swimming away. Charles Williams, a passenger claims that he saw "Captain Smith swimming around the icy water with an infant in his arms and a lifebelt". When the small boat Mr. Williams was in went to rescue Captain Smith, he handed them the child, but refused to get in himself. Then Captain Smith pushed himself away from the lifeboat, threw his lifebelt from him and slowly sank from sight. "He did not come to the surface again." Fireman Harry Senior stated that he saw Smith rescue a child.

Following the popular belief for the final moments of Captain Smith, he then entered the bridge and closed the door to the wheelhouse where he awaited his fate.

A report in the *New York Times* on April 19, 1912, mentions Dr. J.F Kemp, a passenger onboard *Carpathia*. Dr J.F Kemp was a surgeon of the University of the Philippines at Manila. He claimed he was talking to a child on the deck of *Carpathia*: "A boy and one of the last of the children to be taken from the *Titanic* told me that he saw Captain Smith put a pistol to his head then fall down." When asked by the reporter if he believes this story, Kemp replied: "Of course, I cannot tell whether the boy told me the truth, but it seems to me hard to believe the little fellow would invent such a tale. I was talking with him on the deck of the *Carpathia* when he voluntarily told me."

A story told in the *Baltimore, Md* press on 20 July 1912, presents a more ominous account on Captain Smith. Reporting an account by Captain Peter Pryal, who claimed to be a good friend of Smith, stated:

"Captain Pryal, one of the oldest mariners in Baltimore and well known in shipping circles, who sailed with Captain Smith when he was the commander of the *Majestic*, made the startling statement today that he saw and talked to Captain Smith at Baltimore & St. Paul Streets. He declares he walked up to Captain Smith and said, 'Captain Smith, how are you?' Then the man answered, 'Very well, Pryal, but please don't detain me, I am on business.' He says he followed the man, saw him buy a ticket for Washington, and as he passed through the gate of the railway station he turned, recognized Pryal again, and remarked 'Be good, shipmate, until we meet again.' 'There is no possibility of my being mistaken,' said Captain Pryal, 'I have known Captain Smith too long. I would know him even without his beard. I firmly believe that he was saved and in some mysterious manner brought to this country. I am willing to swear to my statement. Many persons may think I am insane, but I have told Dr. Warfield of the occurrence and he will vouch for my sanity.' Dr. Warfield said that Captain Pryal was perfectly sane. The captain is well-to-do and is a consistent church member."

~ ~ ~ ~

Onboard *Carpathia*, Captain Rostron was becoming concerned over the experience for the survivors at the hands of the awaiting press onshore. As the questions were surely going to flow, the survivors would be expected to relive their experiences over and over again. He imagined the difficulties that would bring, as Rostron had been fearful of any false information around the foundering of *Titanic*. He was aware of the rumours circulating onboard from the grief-stricken passengers. Rostron summed up his feelings well at the U.S Senate Inquiry, when Senator Smith asked him about the information being held back by *Carpathia* in the days up till her arrival in New York. In particular, the force of the impact which wrecked the *Titanic*. Rostron said "I know nothing about it, sir. I have not asked any questions about this kind of business. I knew it was not my affair, and I had little desire to make any of the officers feel it any more than they did. Mind you sir, there is only this: I know nothing, but I have heard rumors of different passengers; some will say one thing and some another. I would, therefore, rather say nothing. I do not know anything. From the officers I know nothing. I could give you silly rumors of passengers, but I know they are not reliable, from my own experience; so, if you will excuse me, I would prefer to say nothing."

Top Left and Right - Crowds gather to watch Carpathia enter New York.

Bottom Left - Titanic lifeboats lowered half way prior to offloading at Pier 59.

Bottom Right - Titanic lifeboats at White Star Lines Pier 59.

While approaching New York, wireless operator Harold Cottam was working feverishly with *Titanic* wireless operator, survivor Harold Bride, to dispatch the many messages from survivors to relatives and loved ones onshore. They had both been working non-stop for three days, confusing those waiting onshore. *Carpathia's* wireless was transmitting all day, everyday.

But, no news about the actual sinking of *Titanic* was being transmitted to a waiting world. All requests for information were simply ignored. Survivor, Margaret Brown had personally paid the fee for survivors who could not afford to send messages to loved ones and who would undoubtedly be worrying about their fate.

The heavy fog had lifted as *Carpathia* entered New York Harbour, but heavy rain was falling as she sailed past the statue of Liberty. The rain was accompanied with thunder as she proceeded to the Cunard Lines Pier.

Around 30,000 to 40,000 people had gathered on vantage points around the harbour to watch the great mystery ship. Spectators and reporters were on tug boats, ferries and yachts, escorting her into port and many reporters were offering money for the survivors accounts on the disaster - the story that had captured the world's attention and triggered a flood of intrigue.

As she sailed up the harbour, a tug boat got alongside her, loaded with photographers. The continued flashing of the cameras lit up the side of the ship, revealing the decks were crammed with passengers.

Carpathia, heroically sailed past Pier 54. Her destination was the White Star Lines, Pier 59, the Pier *Titanic* would have occupied before her return voyage to Southampton on April 20 1912.

A message was sent to White Star, informing the company that *Titanic's* lifeboats were hung halfway to the water from davits and asking if tugs could be sent out to take them away, as *Carpathia* could not dock while the boats were onboard. *Titanic's* lifeboats were then offloaded at their home, at White Star Line, Pier 59.

Carpathia then sailed down river to her own Pier 54 to offload her booked passengers and her passengers from *Titanic*. Two thousand people waited on the Pier as *Carpathia* maneuvered into her berth, while relatives, friends, medical personnel and government officials waited in almost complete silence. *Carpathia's* engines finally ceased operating as she docked at Pier 54, close by Fourteenth Street, at 9.35pm.

Captain Rostron knew the attention was going to be placed on the survivors as they disembarked from the vessel, so Rostron allowed *Carpathia's* passengers to disembark first.

Then the moment he feared had come. The scene quickly became frantic as the first *Titanic* survivor headed down the gangway, onto the Pier - a young woman, dressed in make shift clothing, with teary eyes walked down the gangway.

She was then escorted on the arm of an officer, as the waiting crowd finally gave voice to their feelings and wailed with sounds of sobbing and shrieks.

Every man, woman and child who descended the gangways, each had a story to tell. The world wanted to know those stories, every little detail was hounded by the waiting army of press reporters and cameramen. The first glimmer to spark the imagination of the horror and romance came from wireless operator, Harold Bride.

Top Left – Carpathia at pier 54. Bottom Left – Titanic wireless operator, Harold Bride is assisted off Carpathia.

Right – Illustration depicting the sad scene in New York as Titanic survivors disembark Carpathia.

Still nursing his broken and heavily bandaged feet, Bride recounted, the pressure when he was still sending CQD and S. O. S messages, then his eventual departure from the foundering liner. He said: "The way the band kept playing was a noble thing. I heard it first while still we were working wireless when there was a ragtime tune for us, and the last I saw of the band, when I was floating out in the sea with my lifebelt on, it was still on deck playing '*Autumn*.' How they ever did it I cannot imagine."

The men who survived came under scrutiny as they were forced to explain why they managed to survive, when so many women and children died. Perhaps seeded by popular news articles, ostracizing White Star line general manager Ismay.

As is with many major disasters, *Titanic* certainly had its share of stories of heroism, such as that of 36 year old Edith Evans. As they were waiting to board collapsible lifeboat D. Edith turned to fellow passenger, Caroline Brown, then said "You go first. You have children waiting at home" Evan's decision to wait cost her her life. Mrs Brown later exclaimed: "It was a heroic sacrifice, and as long as I live I shall hold her memory dear as my preserver, who preferred to die so I might live."

13 year old, Madeleine Mellinger, had been very excited to be on the greatest ship ever built, which she saw as a symbol of progress, a sign of new beginnings. Along with her Mother, Elizabeth, she was on her way to a new life in North America. While watching *Titanic* from her lifeboat, she recounted "I could see the lights of the ship starting to go under water, then soundlessly, perhaps a mile away, it just went down. It was gone. Oh yes, the sky was very black and the stars were very bright. They told me the people in the water were singing, but I knew they were screaming."

A woman who made herself well known on *Titanic*, made a comment to a reporter's question that completely immortalised the way the world knows her as a famous *Titanic* survivor, Margaret Brown. When asked how she survived the sinking, Margaret replied "Typical Brown luck, We're unsinkable", from that moment onwards, she has been known as "the unsinkable Molly Brown."

Confusion around the exact number of people aboard *Titanic* after the disaster was evident in events that followed *Carpathia's* arrival in New York. Newspapers were reporting the number at 2,340 souls onboard. The exact number given at the U.S. Senate Committee enquiry was recorded at 2,223. Later, however, the British Board of Trade enquiry had the number, using records provided by the White Star Line, at 2,201.

Some supposed passengers and crew were mourned for a few years, before the truth was realised. Miss Eva Wilkinson arrived at her Mothers house in England, sixteen years after she missed her sailing. Not realising her name was still on the passenger list, she managed to get to the United States, where she served as a nurse during World War 1. Thomas Hart was rather too embarrassed to come forward after realising his name was on the list of the dead. His excuse was that he missed the sailing after getting drunk. Almost a month after the disaster, he also appeared at his Mothers house on May 8, 1912.

Several crew members appeared on the list of crew, even though they were not onboard. Three brothers, with their surname as Slade, were sacked on the day of sailing from Southampton, after turning up for duty, drunk. Their names were not taken off the crew list. Fireman John Coffey deserted the ship while anchored at Queenstown, Ireland.

Not mentioning those passengers who missed the sailing due to various reasons, as mentioned earlier in Chapter 3. Some further passengers sailed under assumed names, because luxury liners were known to attract gamblers and con-artists - such as George Brereton, whose real name was George Brayton.

Over a century since *Titanic* sailed into history, modern researchers now give the total number of passengers, Officers and crew onboard *Titanic* at the time of leaving her last port of call, Queenstown, Ireland, as being 2,207 to 2,208.

Conclusion

What do you think I am? Do you believe that I'm the sort that would have left that ship as long as there were any women and children on board? That's the thing that hurts, and it hurts all the more because it is so false and baseless. I have searched my mind with deepest care, I have thought long over each single incident that I could recall of that wreck. I'm sure that nothing wrong was done; that I did nothing that I should not have done. My conscience is clear and I have not been a lenient judge of my own acts.

- J. Bruce Ismay, Director, White Star Line.

On a calm, freezing cold, moonless night, *Titanic* struck an iceberg and consequently, sank after reaching an extreme ice field on her Trans-Atlantic maiden voyage from Southampton to New York. Many stories remain, claiming she was traveling at top speed. Captain Smith failed to heed many ice warnings while determined to reach New York ahead of time, failed to order his ship to slow down on her progression through the adherent danger in front of his ship.

It is not completely clear exactly how many warnings of icebergs *Titanic* had received. Some authors and writers have put that number as six, many four or five. It is, however factual that *Titanic* had received at least three warnings from other steamers, following the southern tract of the North Atlantic on the 14 April 1912. It is debatable if Captain Smith was fully aware of the danger in front of him. But would he have slowed the ship down even if he did fully realise the importance of the warnings?

The beginning of the twentieth century was a time of dramatic changes. The North Atlantic shipping routes saw one of those dramatic changes. Just fifty years previously, Paddle steamers made the crossing from Europe to America in six weeks. A journey which Christopher Columbus took ninety days to complete. Now, in 1912, fast, luxurious steamers were sailing that distance in just four days. Many Trans-Atlantic passengers got quite grumpy with some angry scenes onboard, if they were delayed and their time of arrival was later than expected.

Advertising for the Trans-Atlantic shipping lines were stating: "Leave New York on Wednesday, dine in London the following Monday". The traveling public, were expecting that in greater numbers. The North Atlantic shipping lanes were becoming the North Atlantic express lanes as far as the public was concerned. The traveling public, were increasingly expecting to depart on time and reach their destination on time, in the shortest possible time.

Earlier in this book, you read about assumed literary works, predicting the *Titanic* disaster. Those predictions all have only one theme in common with *Titanic* - large ships, with only enough lifeboat capacity for half her company of passengers and crew. *Titanic* had enough lifeboats to satisfy the British Board Of Trade regulations. Unfortunately, the maritime regulations had not kept pace with reality and with the demands of Trans-Atlantic travel. No Trans-Atlantic passenger mail steamer of that time carried enough lifeboats for the ship's full capacity of passengers and crew. Even shortly after *Titanic* collided with the iceberg, the main belief among the crew, officers and passengers was the vessel would remain afloat for at least one day, allowing all those onboard to be safely off-loaded onto rescue ships, using the lifeboats provided to ferry them between vessels.

The Captain of a vessel is directly, personally responsible for the safety of his ship. He is responsible for his crew's actions. He is responsible for his passengers and the running of the ship. Many Captains had run the gauntlet of the North-Atlantic shipping lanes. The chances of any mail steamer striking an iceberg was, practically non existent, considering the very little space an iceberg presents in the vast area of the North Atlantic Ocean. Insurance companies put the risk of a vessel colliding with an iceberg as a one in a million chance.

Captain Smith would have had no idea of the size of the ice field his ship was steadily approaching on the night of the 14 April 1912.

Many Captains had taken the gamble of running at top speed through fields of ice before. Captain Smith took that gamble, - as he had many times before - and lost, unaware that his chances were far less than one in a million, because of the sheer size of the ice danger. Although he had received some warnings of ice, it is very unlikely that Smith knew the size of that ice field and the numbers of bergs in his ships vicinity. He had no idea his 'ordinary risk' would be so extraordinary.

The story of *Titanic* continues to outrage many, especially the fact that Captain Smith did not slow his ship after he had received warnings of ice. Many other ships could travel much faster than *Titanic* was capable of. If they had struck an iceberg, the impact plus velocity would have ensured far greater damage than *Titanic* suffered. The timetable of these ships and their passengers' expectations of arriving on time virtually ensured that they had to go at full speed at all times.

Was Captain Smith to blame for the loss of *Titanic*? It must be remembered that custom is dictated by demand. The traveling public, were demanding faster, more luxurious travel. The faster, more luxurious vessels were gaining supremacy in the North-Atlantic, over the slower ships of the lines. It's fair to say that the unconscious judgement of any Captain could be swayed toward the illusion of safety, while taking risks that the other smaller, slower ships would not be capable of.

The American press enjoyed criticizing the White Star Line, in particular, J. Bruce Ismay for regulations that dated back from 1894, in their effort to find a scapegoat for the *Titanic* sinking. The British Board Of Trade, were ruthless at ensuring British Ships adhered to their regulations. *Titanic*, prior to departure from Southampton had undergone stringent inspections from Board Of Trade inspectors, to an extent that some Officers had regarded them as, becoming a nuisance. It has to be remembered that, the British built mail steamers, operating the North-Atlantic shipping lanes carried large numbers of Americans. It is governments that should ensure their citizens are safe, especially while at sea. That is why they are in office, that is why they are paid, America allowed the British vessels entry into their ports. The American maritime regulations dictated that vessels the size of *Titanic* should carry twice as many lifeboats as the British vessels. Yet, American authorities allowed British vessels, in defiance of their own laws and carrying large numbers of Americans, entry into their ports.

Lifeboats could be provided at very low cost. *Titanic's* owner, The Mercantile Marine Company, owned by J P Morgan had instructed Ismay and *Titanic's* builder, Harland and Wolff to spare no cost at building the largest, most luxurious vessels afloat. It does not stand to reason that Harland and Wolff or White Star Line would skimp on cost in the provision of life saving equipment for *Titanic* and *Olympic*. The Mercantile Marine Company was an American company, yet, they agreed with the British Board Of Trade regulations, dictating the allowed number of lifeboats for *Titanic*. In all fairness, America should also bear the blame for the loss of *Titanic* with a great number of deaths, especially the large number of American victims, their own maritime regulations were designed to protect.

The insight of *Carpathia's* Captain, Arthur Rostron, clearly displays his knowledge of how simple rumours can turn into what is regarded by many to be "an accurate account". A rumour is a story that is passed around verbally, containing mostly conjecture, based mostly on truths and half-truths. And, some aspects that have simply been interpreted by another, then verbally passed onto others, as truth.

From the time the survivors of the *Titanic* disaster were brought aboard *Carpathia*, Rostron did not wish wireless messages to be sent to the throngs of reporters demanding information of the sinking of the greatest liner at that time, through fear they would cause unnecessary concern for loved ones and the survivors themselves. *Carpathia* was being bombarded with wireless messages, but Rostron remained resolute - any messages sent from his ship would have to be authorised by him and him alone.

The waiting media did however manage to get some news from these messages.

Survivors were sending messages to shore stations, intended for relatives and loved ones, containing small snippets of information that were interpreted by the waiting media who managed to get the information - Information that was partial, to say the least, then, interpreting and adapting that information to what they believed their readers wanted to hear. As a result, many different stories and versions of those stories were being circulated.

Today in the 21st Century, anyone following these stories from different news agencies, via internet would be very confused, to say the least. Back in 1912, however, newspaper accounts were followed by thousands, even millions of readers.

Following a great disaster, such as the *Titanic* disaster, readers liked to believe, what they are reading is the truth, and nothing but the truth. With all the different papers in 1912 reporting different stories and different variations of stories, is it any wonder the *Titanic* tragedy fell into legend?

A legend - deriving from the Latin word, legenda - is a story that has been passed down through time - regarded as historical. The story does contain aspects that are not verifiable. Not verifiable because, some aspects of the *Titanic* disaster includes aspects that are based solely on rumour, also passed down through time. Rumours that have their origins with the news reports from April 1912, and the accounts from the survivors themselves. Stories that are regarded as historical, but contain aspects of truths and untruths, that are solely based on the origins of rumours, are called myths.

A myth is a traditional story - legend - that always has a hero. Therefore, a story also, according to tradition, has to have a villain. The American newspaper tycoon, W Randolph Hearst created a villain contained in the *Titanic* story, in his yellow journalism style of reporting, commonly regarded in the 21st Century as Gutter Journalism. Hearst's Villain? J Bruce Ismay. Simply resulting from an earlier disagreement between the two men, over two decades earlier in New York.

Hearst blamed the entire disaster and the problems during the aftermath, solely on Ismay, without a shred of evidence in support of his allegations against Ismay. *Titanic* stories today always portray Ismay as the coward, who deserted the sinking ship, leaving many men, women and children to die.

Similar aspects of the *Titanic* story, even now, claim *Titanic* was "unsinkable". Obviously, *Titanic* was not unsinkable. Because, she sank after colliding side on with an iceberg. opening up five of her watertight compartments to the water, totally compromising her 'practically unsinkability'. The legends and myths surrounding the *Titanic* story enter the realm of folklore.

Folklore comprises collections of popular stories, containing legend, myths and oral history - All the aspects contained in the *Titanic* story, passed on from generation to generation, through many books written on the subject and movies telling the story. But, unfortunately, also containing the legends and myths.

The 1958 movie adaptation of Walter Lord's book, '*A Night To Remember*' is an example of the tragedy of the sinking of *Titanic*, although, alas, it also has its content of the associated myths.

James Cameron's 1997 movie "*Titanic*" is a classic example of all three aspects, containing the legend, myths and folklore. It has its villain and hero. And, as if as a bonus, it also contains the actual story of *Titanic*, all nicely wrapped up into a parcel of love and romance, with the backdrop of Cameron's portrayal of Hell on Earth.

The story of *Titanic* and the events that sent her to the bottom of the Atlantic Ocean on 14 to 15 April 1912 has come a long way from its origins of truth and rumour. The day after the rescue ship, *Carpathia* berthed in New York, carrying the surviving passengers of the grand liner, the U. S. Senate inquiry began in New York at the Waldorf-Astoria Hotel, on the 19 April, 1912. On the first day of proceedings, Captain Arthur Rostron was questioned about *Titanic*, herself. Rostron repeatedly told Senator Alden Smith that he did not know anything about *Titanic*, because he had no experience with her. Senator Smith asked him another question regarding *Titanic*. Smith asked: "Have you any kind of knowledge at all regarding the force of the impact, which wrecked *Titanic*?"

Rostron simply replied; "I know nothing about it, sir. I have not asked any questions about this kind of business. I knew it was not my affair, and I had little desire to make any of the officers feel it any more than they did. Mind you sir, there is only this: I know nothing, but I have heard rumors of different passengers; some will say one thing and some another. I would, therefore, rather say nothing. I do not know anything. From the officers I know nothing. I could give you silly rumors of passengers, but I know they are not reliable, from my own experience; so, if you will excuse me, I would prefer to say nothing."

The *Titanic* legend is a story based on truth. The story also includes its traditional aspects, it contains its heroes and villains. The lasting story does contain parts that are solely based on rumour. Parts that do not belong to such a sad and tragic event that claimed the lives of real people and the suffering of real survivors and those left behind by so much death and destruction that captivated a generation, so many years ago.

The story of *Titanic* deserves its place in history. It was a time of innocence. A time when overnight, the world awoke to realise the true impact of what can happen when man decides to take on the power of nature. Our world has changed since 1912. We now design ocean vessels that are substantially safer through lessons learnt from *Titanic* and technological advances since then.

I will end this book with one question: How do you extract the legends, myths and folklore from the story of *Titanic*? Surely, that's up to the reader, listener or viewer of such stories to determine for themselves.

Appreciation

I would personally like to thank you for purchasing and reading this book. I enjoyed writing **TITANIC - The Legend, Myths and Folklore**. I hope it was enjoyable for you to read.

Index

The Construction....21

Worker Trapped In Titanic Hull…………..23

390904 = No Pope…

The Fitting Out……37

Big Gash In The Side Of Titanic…………...…38

Unsinkable………...46

Sea Trials…………..51

Literary Predictions.58

Arthur Paintin……..59

W. T. Stead………...60

The Wreck Of The Titan, Or Futility………....62

Steerage Passengers Blocked Access To Lifeboats……………….73

Titanic's Mummy...86

Coal Bunker Fire…98

The Ship That Never Sank…………..……..104

No Binoculars………109

The Haze, An Optical Illusion…………………..124

Titanic Was Attempting A Speed Record……..140

Lifeboats………….143

Nearer My God To Thee……………....168

The Breakup……..185

J. Bruce Ismay…...192

The Telephone Rang For A Few Minutes……201

First Officer William Murdoch Shot Himself……………….214

The Hero - Captain E.J. Smith…………….233

What Happened To Smith?…………...236

TITANIC: The Legend, Myths and Folklore

Bruce Alpine

ePub ISBN: 978-1-301-20346-8

Print ISBN: 978-0-9941053-9-4

www.ingramcontent.com/pod-product-compliance
Lightning Source LLC
LaVergne TN
LVHW051547070426
835507LV00021B/2454